32367
B/MAU | BOYD | Guy de Maupassant

Please renew/return this item by the last date shown.

So that your telephone call is charged at local rate,
please call the numbers

From Area codes
01923 or 020:

Renewals: 01923 4713
Enquiries: 01923 471333   01438 737333
Minicom: 01923 471599   01438 737599

L32b

D1180854

GUY DE MAUPASSANT
A BIOGRAPHICAL STUDY

GUY DE MAUPASSANT

A Biographical Study

by

ERNEST BOYD

"*Bourget, Maupassant et Loti
Se trouvent dans toutes les gares,
D'eux soyez nanti
Ainsi que de cigares.*"

LAURENT TAILHADE

London

ALFRED · A · KNOPF

Mcmxxvi

PRINTED IN THE UNITED STATES OF AMERICA

A MA FEMME.

En souvenir de notre Normandie
qui était celle de Maupassant.

CONTENTS

ILLUSTRATIONS

CHAPTER I

THE AGE OF INNOCENCE

IN 1850 the subconscious could still call its private life its own, and psychoanalysis had not yet enabled dirty souls to be decorously washed in public. It was possible, therefore, for Madame Laure Le Poittevin de Maupassant to insist complacently that none but she had ever nursed her first-born, Henri René Albert Guy de Maupassant, and that her darling boy had not been weaned until he was more than eighteen months old. She did not thereby invite any of the insinuations which that fact, coupled with certain peculiarities of her son's subsequent career, would at once suggest to an alert psychologist of to-day. At the time when Napoleon the Small was making up the uncertain mind of the Second French Republic, by preparing to pronounce it a Second Empire, simpler preoccupations engaged public attention and governed private conduct. Madame de Maupassant's boast was regarded as but the becoming expression of her motherly pride in her children, by way of compensation for what her old friend Gustave Flaubert called "the platitudes of marriage," in a novel which startled Paris the year her second and last child, Hervé, was born.

In 1846 Laure Le Poittevin and her brother Alfred had married, much to the disgust of Flaubert, who wrote to a friend from his retreat at Croisset: "Here everybody is going away and leaving me, even my servant, who doubtless finds me too dull and craves more amusing society. Alfred is married, as you know; he is in Italy with his wife. On his return he will live in Paris. His sister has married his wife's brother. It is raining marriages; the barometer is at stormy." And thus was broken up the charming circle of friends from childhood, the Flauberts and the Le Poittevins, whose memory remained with Flaubert to the end of his days, and was to be the bond between Laure de Maupassant and himself, when she at last turned back to him for comfort and advice. With the brilliant, wayward, and bawdy Alfred correspondence was exchanged until the latter's death in 1848. Of all this there remains a much censored and recently published volume to persuade an age that has forgotten him that there must have been something in the man who was Flaubert's dearest friend and to whom *La Tentation de Saint Antoine* was dedicated.

With her two sons Laure de Maupassant filled in her days and nights at Étretat, at Yvetot, in Paris, while her gay young dandy of a husband, Gustave de Maupassant, occupied himself with such pursuits as were natural to a handsome gentleman of the old school, such as Bellange has painted in the portrait of him that hangs in the Rouen Museum. Laure remembered what Gustave Flaubert and Alfred Le Poittevin had been to her as a child, and she set about giving Guy and Hervé the rudiments of an education, in which their father seems to have shown little interest. When Guy was about ten, the Lycée Impérial Napoléon in Paris expressed its official satisfaction with the results of her tuition. "An excellent pupil, whose determination and efforts deserve the highest praise and encouragement. Gradually he will get accustomed to our methods of work and we are confident he will make progress."

Unfortunately, Guy's communications were couched in less formal language. "I was first in composition. As a reward Madame de X. took me to the circus with papa. It seems papa is also being rewarded for something, but I don't know what." Whereupon it dawned upon the mother that the one thing which she did not want her boys to learn from their father was beginning to have a great interest for the precocious Guy. When the two youngsters were invited to a children's party given by one of the estimable ladies who enjoyed the confidence of Gustave de Maupassant, Laure decided to stay at home and nurse Hervé, who was not well enough to go. The father did not hesitate to offer his services as a chaperon for Guy, and while the latter dressed, he concealed his impatience as best he could under an air of paternal benevolence:

"If you don't hurry up, we'll be late for the party."

"What do I care? It is you who want to go there most, not me."

"Come along now. Tie your laces."

"No. You tie them. You know you will sooner or later, so do it now." And the defenceless parent felt he could refuse his son nothing.

Laure de Maupassant, however, decided that so wicked an example as that of their father must no longer threaten the virtue of her sons, and in 1862 the parents separated in a friendly way. The control of her fortune reverted to the mother, and the father paid an allowance annually for his two children until he lost all his own property. Whereupon Gustave de Maupassant set to work, in defiance of all his family traditions, and made quite a little career for himself in banking, so that in the end he again achieved the French Nirvana, and became once more a *rentier* and a gentleman. At no time could even Guy's adoration of his mother induce him to adopt any but an attitude of friendly respect towards that elusive father of his, who disappears from his life as the boy enters his teens and, but for one brief period at the outset of his career in Paris, reappears only after the catastrophe has happened for which he would certainly have been blamed had the parents remained together, for destiny had certainly determined to demonstrate that it is easier to drive out a father than to extirpate human instincts. The records, however, solemnly and reassuringly declare that "it was not until he was sixteen years old" that Maupassant became acquainted with "the degrading passion of love," to quote the words of an Irish Bishop. Up to that time his life had been "pure," thanks to the eternal vigilance, presumably, of his anxious mother.

By the time he was thirteen, however, the desultory education which he had been receiving was deemed insufficient, and he was dispatched from Étretat to the Institution Ecclésiastique at the neighbouring village of Yvetot, more renowned in Béranger's song than for its learning or piety. Here the boy was frankly unhappy. His instinctive rationalism had been encouraged by his mother, and he declared years later that "even as a small boy religious rites and ceremonies offended me. I could see only their ridiculous side." In this stronghold of the Norman squirearchy, where the stolid offspring of prosperous farmers and country gentlemen were confirmed in the prejudices of their class and the superstitions of their ancestors, Maupassant keenly resented both the physical restraints of his restricted existence and the religious discipline in which the institution was steeped. He began to write his first verses, of which some specimens have been preserved.

La vie est le sillon du vaiseau qui s'éloigne,
C'est l'éphémère fleur qui croît sur la montagne,
C'est l'ombre de l'oiseau qui traverse l'éther,
C'est le cri du marin englouti par la mer...
La vie est un brouillard qui se change en lumière,
C'est l'unqiue moment donné pour la prière

They do credit to the talent of a child of thirteen and explain why the first report of his teachers indicated a model pupil. "*Conduct:* orderly, *Work:* regular, *Character:* good, obedient, and diligent; popular with everybody."

One day, however, when he was overheard parodying a sermon on eternal damnation, he was warned that he could be expelled for less. Whereupon he decided to make his exit in a cloud of glorious obloquy. He inscribed a poem to a young lady, in words more or less to the following effect:

Comment relégué loin du monde,
Privé de l'air, des champs, des bois,
Dans la tristesse qui m'inonde
Faire entendre une douce voix?

Vous m'avez dit: « Chantez des fêtes
Où les fleurs et les diamants
S'enlacent sur le blondes têtes,
Chantez le bonheur des amants. »

Mais dans le cloître solitaire
Où nous sommes ensevelis
Nous ne connaîssons sur la terre
Que soutanes et que surplis.

Pauvres exilés que nous sommes
Il faut chanter des biens si doux
Et du bonheur des autres hommes
Ne jamais nous montrer jaloux!

Un poète est donc insensible?
Pour lui l'amour n'a point d'appas?
Non, voyez-vous, c'est impossible!
Oh! ne vous imaginez pas

Que dans le cloître solitaire
Où nous sommes ensevelis,
Nous n'aspirions plus sur la terre
Qu'aux soutanes et qu'aux surplis!

Finissons, de peur de déplaire,
En vous parlant de mon malheur...
L'avenir que pour vous j'espère
Est plaisir, amour et bonheur.

Gardez bien cette heureuse ivresse
Et cueillez les fleurs du chemin;
Mais parfois plaignez ma jeunesse
En vous disant que le chagrin

Reste en ce cloître solitaire
Où nous sommes ensevelis,
Et que l'on n'y voit sur la terre
Que soutanes et que surplis.

Here was heresy coupled with positive incitements to fleshly sin. The author was deemed as dangerous for Yvetot's rising youth as Gustave de Maupassant had been deemed dangerous for the precocious author. The crime was further complicated by an escapade in which the pupils, under Maupassant's leadership, revenged themselves for the bad wine served to them at meals. When the masters were asleep the keys to the cellar were appropriated and a fine selection of the best wines and old brandy was transported to the roof of the school. There a mighty feast was celebrated until about four A.M., when the exuberance of spirit engendered by these libations began to make itself heard and aroused the sleeping pedagogues. As the respon-

Gustave de Maupassant
from a portrait by Bellangé in the Rouen Museum

sible ringleader, Maupassant was expelled from the school. Thus Guy de Maupassant was restored to his mother's care by the indignant but puzzled authorities, who uttered their conviction in a final report: "Still a good, attractive pupil." Whereat Madame de Maupassant received the prodigal and told him he would go, instead, to the Lycée at Rouen.

Shortly after her separation from her husband, Laure de Maupassant had received a letter from Flaubert, which was like a breath of old times, and which she had often reread: "Your kind letter," he wrote, "has aroused in me old feelings that are always young. Like a breath of fresh air, it brought back all the perfume of my youth, in which our dear Alfred held such a place. His memory never leaves me. There is not a day nor an hour in which I do not think of him. Now I know what people are pleased to call 'the most intelligent men of the day.' When I measure them by him, they all seem mediocre by comparison. Not one of them has ever amazed me the way your brother used to do. What voyages into the empyrean we used to take, and how I loved him! I can believe I have never loved any one (man or woman) like him. When he married I was filled with a deep, jealous sorrow. It was a break and a tear. For me, he died twice, and I wear the thought of him like an amulet, something intimate and one's very own. Many a time when I am tired after my work, at the theatre, in Paris, during an interval, or alone at home at Croisset, I turn back to him, I can see and hear him again. I remember with delight and sorrow our endless conversations, intermingled with jokes and metaphysics, our reading, our dreams, and our high aspirations. If I am worth anything, it is to that I owe it. I have preserved a great respect for that past. It was very fine and I wanted to keep up to that level.

"I can see you all in your house in the Grande Rue, when you used to walk in the sunshine on the terrace beside the aviary. As soon as I arrived the 'boy's' laughter broke forth. How I should like to talk over old times with you, dear Laure. It is so long since we have seen each other. But I have followed your doings from a distance and shared your sorrows, which I guessed. I 'understood' you, in a word, an old word, a word of our time, a good old word of the Romantic school. It says exactly what I want to say, so I keep it.

"Since you mention *Salammbô*, you will be glad to hear that my 'Carthaginian Lady' is getting along in the world: my publisher announces a second edition on Friday. All the papers are talking about me. I am making them talk a great deal of nonsense. Some run me down, others praise me to the sky. I have been called 'a drunken Helot'; told that I spread 'an infected atmosphere'; compared to Châteaubriand and Marmontel. I have been accused of aiming at the Academy, and one lady who read the book has asked if Fanit was not a devil. There is literary glory! First you are mentioned from time to time, than you are forgotten, and then all is over.

"However, I wrote a book for a limited circle of readers, and the public seems to like it. May the bookselling gods be praised! I was very glad you liked it, for you know how highly I esteem your intelligence, my dear Laure. We are not only friends since childhood, but fellow-students, almost. Do you remember how we used to read *Les Feuilles d'Automne* at Fécamp, in the little room on the second floor? . . .

"Kiss your boys from me, my dear Laure, with a long handshake and best thoughts from your old friend."

When old Madame Le Poittevin died, early in 1866, Flaubert and Laure de Maupassant were brought still closer by their common grief, and when she came to acknowledge his letter of condolence, Laure decided to tell Flaubert about her son, Guy.

"At present I must force myself to think of the future. I have two children whom I love with all my strength, and they perhaps will bring me some happiness before I die. The younger just now is nothing more than a fine little peasant lad, but the elder is already a serious young gentleman. The poor boy has seen and understood many things and is almost too mature for his fifteen years. He will remind you of his Uncle Alfred, whom he resembles in many ways, and I am sure you will like him. I have just been obliged to take him away from the Ecclesiastical Institute at Yvetot, where they refused to grant him a dispensation from fasting ordered by his doctors — which is a strange way, it seems to me, of understanding the teaching of Christ! . . . My son is not seriously ill, but he is suffering from nervous debility, which requires a tonic diet, and, besides, he did not like the place. The austerity of that cloistered life did not suit his sensitive and delicate nature. The poor child was stifled behind those high walls, which admitted no sound from the outside world. I think I shall send him to the Lycée at Havre for eighteen months, and then I'll go and live in Paris until he is ready to go to the University. Hervé can become a day pupil in some school and so I shall be able to watch over my two darlings myself."

The boy was sent to pay a visit to his mother's old friends, and evidently made a good impression, for Madame de Maupassant received a letter from her former playmate, Flaubert's sister Caroline, who wrote:

"I cannot tell you how much I enjoyed your son's visit. He is a charming boy and you may well be proud of him. He is a little like you and also like our poor dear Alfred. His clever, animated face is very attractive, and his young comrade said he was gifted in every way. Your old friend Gustave is delighted with him and asks me to congratulate you on having such a child."

Laure de Maupassant needed no further proof that her judgment concerning Guy de Maupassant was sound. The Lycée at Havre lacked one attraction which that at Rouen possessed in Flaubert's eyes. At Rouen Guy would come under the influence of his friend Louis Bouilhet, and, accordingly, to Rouen he went. The freer life of that charming old city was more congenial, and not only did his studies progress satisfactorily to the point where he obtained his degree of *Bachelier-ès-lettres*, but he also found time for not unprofitable dalliance with the Muse of calf-love:

> Il fallait la quitter, et pour ne plus me voir
> Elle partait, mon Dieu, c'était le dernier soir.
> Elle me laissait seul: cette femme cruelle
> Emportait mon amour et ma vie avec elle.
> Moi je voulus encore errer comme autrefois
> Dans les champs et l'aimer une dernière fois.
> La nuit nous apportait et l'ombre et le silence,
> Et pourtant j'entendais comme une vie immense,
> Tout semblait animé par une souffle divin.
> La nature tremblait, j'écoutais et soudain
> Un étrange frisson troubla toute mon âme.

Lamartinian strophes which testify to a mood remote from that which eventually inspired his first and only volume of poems.

More important, however, than the tragic loves of the period, or than even the official studies in which

he acquitted himself so well, was the influence upon
him of Rouen's great poet, Louis Bouilhet. One afternoon as the young *lycéen* was walking out in the "croco-
dile" march, in the charge of his Latin teacher, the
latter drew the attention of his pupils to a striking
looking figure, wandering in solitary meditation, lost
in his dreams. The leonine head was crowned with a
mass of fair hair, and under his arm he carried the
notebooks in which he wrote down the poems that
came to him in his exalted reveries. This was Louis
Bouilhet, of whom Guy had heard so much as the
friend of Gustave Flaubert and the object of the latter's
boundless admiration. In their day Bouilhet's dramas
had been the talk of Paris, historical and poetic plays
of an impeccable classical beauty, and his book of
verses, *Festons et Astragales*, was esteemed for the same
high quality of sheer artistry. He wrote Latin with the
same ease as French, was a classical and scientific
scholar, and had studied Chinese for ten years in order
to translate from that language. Rouen looked with
a certain reluctant respect at this distinguished possession, as to whose real worth it was more than a little
dubious. He earned a frugal independence by coaching
pupils for the Lycée examinations and was finally rewarded by a position as city librarian. When he died,
in 1869, Flaubert was heart-broken, and collected a
volume of his *Dernières Chansons* in a final effort to
get recognition for his friend. When the Rouen municipal Council refused to grant a site for a monument to
this illustrious son, to be erected at the expense of his
friends and admirers, Flaubert addressed them in a
philippic which is the classic indictment of the endless
insolence of elected persons.

When Guy de Maupassant saw him he was not satisfied until he had bought a copy of *Festons and Astragales*,

and for a month he was intoxicated by "this exalted and sensitive poetry." In due course he presented himself at the poet's door and made the welcome already awaiting him additionally secure by declaiming the poems of none other than Louis Bouilhet. A close friendship was established and the young writer began to receive his first lessons in literary art and composition from the first author of renown whom he had known intimately. Bouilhet did his best to make a poet out of his young friend. He pointed out repeatedly that a hundred lines, or less, are enough to ensure a poet's reputation, provided they are perfect and contain the essence of the poet's talent and originality, even if these be of second order. Continuous work and complete knowledge of one's craft could produce the unique and perfect masterpiece, if the happy combination of author and subject had occurred under appropriate conditions. Flaubert joined in these discussions and carried away from them a conviction, which he did not abandon for many years, that poetry was Maupassant's real *métier*.

Sometimes Bouilhet and Flaubert took their young disciple on less strenuous expeditions than adventuring in pursuit of perfect literary form. Once he accompanied them to the fair, around which they wandered like two children. Bouilhet gave an impersonation of a Norman peasant and Flaubert acted the rôle of the wife. In dialect they exchanged comments and views illustrating the droll twists and quirks of that stolid Norman character which must have been a hint to Maupassant for many of the unforgettable scenes, incidents, and types which he himself was to elaborate from his own observations of the same people. From both Flaubert and Bouilhet he at once learned to look upon the art of writing as something independent of aesthetic pose and commercial astuteness. Both men had resolutely refrained from all the tricks and compromises of the profession and they made upon him an impression of intellectual and artistic integrity which made it impossible for him all his life to find any other names in modern French literature comparable, in his eyes, to theirs.

Whenever the Lycée released him, Maupassant returned eagerly to his beloved Étretat, there to resume his vagabondage between the wooded Norman valleys and the ever-changing sea. His holidays in the summer of 1868 were particularly entrancing because of the strange tenants from England who had taken a little place at Étretat and given it the sinister name of "La Chaumière de Dolmancé." One of them was a plump little man, of gentle manners, with an almost invisible blond moustache. His diet consisted solely of monkey, boiled, roasted, or *sauté*, and while he spent hours talking aloud to himself, he avoided all human society but that of his friend. He seemed to live in a fantastic dream like another Edgar Allan Poe, and Maupassant dearly longed to see the volume of Icelandic legends which this visitor had translated into English. He loved the supernatural, the macabre, the tortured, and the complicated, all kinds of cerebral perversion, but he spoke of these things with the admirable phlegm and traditional calm of his race, and thus added to his prestige in the eyes of the young French observer.

One day Maupassant heard from this Englishman that his friend had gone out swimming and had almost drowned. He set out in a boat, but was in time only to meet the craft that had just picked up the drowning Englishman, who was seated on the deck, attired only in a sail, declaiming the poems of Hugo and preaching republicanism, his golden hair floating in the breeze. When his clothes were brought to him and the two Englishmen retired to a warm dish of boiled monkey

— presumably — the patience and proffered help of Maupassant were rewarded by the long-awaited invitation to call the next day. And thus he remembered that exciting experience:

"The friend was a young fellow of about thirty, with an enormous head on a child's body — a body without any chest or shoulders to speak of. An immense forehead, which seemed to dominate the rest of the man, rose like a dome over a thin face, which ended in the point of a little beard on his sharp chin. The sharp eyes and receding lips gave the impression of a reptile's head, while the magnificent skull suggested a genius. Nervous shudders kept agitating this strange being, who walked up and down, moved and acted jerkily, as if shaken by a spring that was broken.

"His curious, disturbing face became transfigured when he spoke. I have rarely seen a man more striking, eloquent, incisive, and charming in the act of speech. His quick, clear, superfine, fantastic imagination seemed to creep into his voice, to give nerves and life to his words. His jerky gestures punctuated his erratic sentences, which penetrated to the mind like a point. He had sudden flashes of thought as lighthouses have flashes of light, the white light of genius which lit up a whole world of ideas.

"The house of the two friends was nice and very unusual. There were pictures everywhere, some superb, others strange, recording the visions of madmen. I remember a water-colour representing a skull floating in a pink shell, on a boundless ocean, beneath a moon with a human face. Here and there were heaps of human bones. I was specially struck by an awful hand, which had kept its dried skin, its black muscles exposed, and on the bone, which was as white as snow, were traces of old blood.

"The food was a puzzle to which I had no key. Was it good? Was it bad? I don't know. A roast of monkey took away all desire I might ordinarily have to eat this animal, and the huge ape at liberty, which wandered around us, and jokingly shoved my head into my glass when I tried to drink, took from me all desire to own one of his brothers as a daily companion.

"As for the two men, they impressed me as two singularly original and remarkable minds, completely eccentric, belonging to that race of especially talented madmen which produced Poe, Hoffmann, and many others."

Thus Guy de Maupassant had his first encounter with two Englishmen of letters and was present at the rescue of Algernon Charles Swinburne from drowning. Those who remember his inability in all his writings even approximately to describe an English character, will note the beginnings here of that talent for misrepresentation. Flaubert and Bouilhet and George Powell and Swinburne were evidently too much for one *lycéen* in a single year. By the time the Franco-Prussian War was over, the young writer had acquired a further set of first impressions which stood in lieu of observation, so far as another foreign race was concerned, for the rest of his life.

In Rouen as elsewhere in the first months of 1870, the general feeling was that war would come. The year had been a bad one for Flaubert, as he complained. Bouilhet, Sainte-Beuve, and Jules de Goncourt had died, and it was in vain that he tried to settle down to work on *La Tentation de Saint Antoine*. Finally, when war was declared, he became a medical attendant at the Hôtel Dieu, pending the time, as he wrote to Edmond de Goncourt, "when I shall have to go and defend Lutetia, if it is besieged (which I doubt)." The disorder, the disorganization, and the futility of the whole adventure filled him with despair. "The winter is going to be charming here," he wrote. "What a fine figure Badinguet is! I am a lieutenant and am training my men. It makes me vomit with disgust when I do not weep with rage. And the worst of it is, we deserve our fate; the Prussians are right, or at least they were right."

After the battle of Sedan, Normandy began to take the war seriously. "A peasant near Mantes has strangled a Prussian and mutilated him with his teeth. In short, the enthusiasm is genuine." In October George Sand heard from Flaubert that "the Prussians are now twelve hours from Rouen, and we have neither order nor leadership nor discipline — absolutely nothing."

By December both illusions and philosophical detachment had become impossible. The Germans had occupied Croisset and Flaubert had moved with his mother into Rouen. Strange to relate, no particular atrocities could be reported. "The Prussians did not loot my home. They stole some unimportant trifles, a toilet-case, a box, some pipes, but on the whole they did no harm. My library was respected. I had buried a huge box full of letters and hidden away all my notes for *Saint Antoine*. I found them all intact. . . . In order to escape from my private and public misfortunes I have plunged furiously into *Saint Antoine*, and if I am not disturbed and can continue like this, I shall have finished next winter. . . .

"The only reasonable thing (I always come back to this) is a government of mandarins, provided the mandarins know something, or even a great deal. The people are the eternal minor, and (in the hierarchy of social elements) they will always be in the last rank, for they represent numbers, the mass, the unlimited. It is of no importance that a lot of peasants should know how to read and then defy the parish priest. It is of the utmost importance that many men like Renan or Littré should live and obtain a hearing. Now our safety lies in a *real aristocracy*, I mean a majority consisting of something more than figures. . . . Ah, how much more practical it would have been to keep Badinguet, in order to send him to the hulks as soon as peace was declared! . . .

When General von Goeben had entered Rouen in December, young Maupassant was one of the army that retreated before him amid such scenes as he afterwards described in *Boule de Suif*. In a letter to his mother he gave an account of his own escape:

"I fled with our army in retreat. I was almost captured. I went from the front to the rear to carry an order from the commissariat to the General. I did *fifteen leagues on foot*. After having marched and run all the preceding night delivering orders, I slept on the stones in an icy cellar. If I had not had a good pair of legs, they would have captured me. I ran very well."

From Paris, however, affairs began to look more promising to the young warrior, who had acquired the national illusions so markedly in contrast with all that his own sharp eyes had observed and his memory treasured up for future use:

"Dear mother: I am writing you a few words more to-day, because within the next forty-eight hours all communication between Paris and the rest of France will be suspended. The Prussians are descending upon us by forced marches. As for the result of the war, it is no longer in doubt. The Prussians are lost. They know it only too well themselves, and their one hope is to capture Paris by surprise, but we are ready to receive them.

"I am not sleeping yet at Vincennes, and am in no hurry to set up my bed there. I prefer to be in Paris during the siege rather than in the old fort down there where we are quartered, for that old fort will be pulverized by the Prussian guns. My father is at his wits' end. He insists on my entering the Commissariat Department of Paris — and he gives me the funniest advice about avoiding accidents. If I were to listen to him, I should apply for a post as guardian of the main drain and thus escape bombs. Robert will be in the firing-line at Saint-Maur. The militia have big guns and do pretty well. Médrinal writes asking me to lend him my Lefaucheux, but I am going to tell him that I have promised it to my cousin Germer. Yesterday Madame Denisane offered me a seat at the Opera. I went to hear 'The Mute of Portici'; it is very pretty.

"Faure-Dujarric, who is a great friend of the head of the Commissariat Department, has offered to do everything he can to find me comfortable quarters. He went to see him yesterday and will go back again to-morrow. Life in barracks is very dull; I should feel better in some of the offices, or in camp, but I should see nobody, as communication with the army has become very difficult.

"Good-bye, Mother dear. I embrace you and Hervé. Remember me to Joseph. Father sends his love to you.
Your son, Guy de Maupassant."

His father's advice, however, was followed, in the end, and Maupassant passed the necessary examinations at Vincennes to be admitted to the Commissariat Department. He was attached to the offices of the Second Division until September, 1871, when, comparative order having been restored by Thiers and Gam-

*The Château de Miromesnil, near Dieppe,
where Maupassant was born*

betta, he procured a substitute, and retired from the
military service of the Third Republic. "For the first
time," as Flaubert remarked, "we are living under a
government which has no principles. . . . Its lack of
elevation is perhaps a guarantee of solidity," and he
became lost in admiration of a certain Mademoiselle
Papavoine, a *pétroleuse*, "who submitted, in the middle
of a barricade, to the assaults of eighteen citizens."
"This," he wrote to George Sand, "puts the end of
L'Éducation sentimentale in the shade, where they
merely offered flowers."

Meanwhile Maupassant had returned to his mother
in Étretat, undecided whether to resume his law studies,
which had been so abruptly terminated by the effort
to think imperially of the Napoleon whom they called
Badinguet. At an impressionable age he had been
given the opportunity to observe types and incidents
which were to receive such immortality as his stories
could give them. He had looked upon the devastation
and futility of war with such objectivity as to describe
its effects upon his own people in *L'Horrible* and *Saint
Antoine*. But *Le Lit 28* showed that he himself was
not immune from the grotesquer forms of patriotism.
The conventions, rather than his imagination, deformed
Le Père Milon, Un Duel, and *La Mère Sauvage*. Yet,
that he had not been blinded to the endless absurdity
of the spectacle of small men confronted with events
too big for them was evident when he came to write
L'Aventure de Walter Schnaffs and *Un Coup d'État*.

To return from the wars with material for two stories
like *Boule de Suif* and *Mlle. Fifi* will seem sufficient
booty for a youth of twenty-one, whatever estimate
be placed upon these most famous of all his war tales.
Adrienne Legay of Rouen, whose adventures inspired
Boule de Suif, protested against Maupassant's version

of the affair. "It is untrue," she said; "it is Monsieur Guy's revenge, because I refused to listen to him. His type did not appeal to me . . . and how was I to know that he would become celebrated? " — a comment which has in it something of the sardonic charm of the story itself. However unfair to Adrienne, her story turned out to be the most valuable asset which Guy de Maupassant brought with him when he so cautiously set out upon the conquest of Paris.

It was the end of his mother's tutelage; now he was transferred to the care of Flaubert, who happened to be spending a great deal of time that winter in Paris. Turgenev had taken a house, and he and Flaubert were meeting weekly, to discuss literature and hear Flaubert read parts of the *Tentation de Saint Antoine.* Every Sunday Maupassant went to Flaubert's, and there he made his first acquaintances in the world of letters: Turgenev, Alphonse Daudet, Zola, and Edmond de Goncourt. For nearly ten years he lived and worked under Flaubert's guidance, submitting everything he wrote to the Master and serving an apprenticeship which, in the eyes of the adoring Laure and her old friend, was bound to be of the utmost importance to the future of French literature. They viewed Maupassant's vocation as seriously as ever the youthful Milton felt the call to be a poet and retire from the world to prepare for his exalted mission. This love of Flaubert for his "adopted son " was the last great friendship of his life, and in the struggles of the young writer for self-expression the Master lived again his own life of disinterested and lofty devotion to the art and craft of French fiction. If there was to be irony and tragedy in the results, Flaubert did not live to know it.

CHAPTER II

THE CAUTIOUS ADVENTURER

HE conquest of Paris by Guy de Maupassant was an adventure undertaken in a spirit of the utmost caution, and without any undue risks. Although his mother felt that her boy took after his Uncle Alfred, and that his literary aspirations should be encouraged, there could be no question of his facing the hazards of literary life in Paris and making his way up from bohemia. The Latin Quarter never knew him as a student, and it was not to know him as *débutant* of letters. A way had to be found whereby Maupassant could safely experiment with his talents and find his destiny, without experiencing any of those picturesque ups and downs of fortune which are, at least in retrospect, the romance of young authorship. It was decided to find him a position in the Government Service, that haven of refuge for all sorts and conditions of Frenchmen.

After one refusal, and a great deal of wire-pulling on the part of his father, Maupassant was assured that an application of his would be favourably received, and on the 20th of February, 1872, he wrote to the Ministry of Marine:

"Monsieur le Ministre,

"I have the honour to solicit a favour from your Excellency, which would be of great value to me: a post in the Ministry of Marine.

"On finishing my studies at the Lycée of Rouen, I received the degree of *bachelier ès lettres* on the 27th of July,

1869. When war was declared against Prussia, I was just
beginning to study law. . . .

"The favour which I am asking Your Excellency to grant
would be all the more valuable in that it would permit me,
I hope, to continue in Paris the studies so suddenly interrupted by the war, without preventing me from discharging
promptly and zealously the duties entrusted to me.

"I have the honour to be,
with the highest respect,
Your Excellency's
most obedient, humble servant,
GUY DE MAUPASSANT."

On the 20th of March, 1872, he was appointed a
temporary clerk and given some vague position in the
library of the Ministry. It was not until the 25th of
January, 1873, that he actually received a permanent
appointment in the printing and stationery department,
where it was his duty to control the supplies of paper
and printed matter furnished by the Imprimerie Nationale to the Ministry. His salary, like that of Hector
Gribelin in À cheval, was 1500 francs a year. His
"intelligence, zeal, and irreproachable conduct " were
duly noted by his chiefs, and in 1876 he sent in an
application for leave with full pay, and was granted
his first holiday in four years. By this time his health
was beginning to be unsatisfactory, as the records
show. "Very delicate, despite his robust appearance,"
wrote the head of his department, "but service satisfactory. . . . He is anxious to do well and to make
himself useful. M. de Maupassant has been on a
salary of 1800 francs for three years. . . . I suggest
his promotion to the 2100-franc scale." In 1877 a
report went forward to the effect that, "according to
medical certificate, M. de Maupassant, third class clerk
in the central office, is ordered to take the waters at
Louèche. . . . M. Sabattier requests the Minister to

grant M. de Maupassant leave with full pay, equivalent to twice the duration of his stay at the baths, but not exceeding two months, according to paragraph 10, sub-section 74, of the Order of January 14, 1869."

The years which he spent at the Ministry of Marine were years of depression, relieved only by the escapades of his holidays and free hours, and, above all, by the friendship and teaching of Flaubert. "Your son," the latter wrote, "is right to be fond of me; because I feel a real friendship for him. He is amusing, well read, and charming. Moreover, he is your son and dear Alfred's nephew." Amongst the letters in which he complains of his ill-tempered chiefs and the contemptible colleagues so often pilloried in his stories, there are always allusions to the consolation of his Sunday boating on the Seine, and to his apprenticeship, under Flaubert, to the career which the latter predicts for him.

"Guy is so happy to go to you every Sunday, to be allowed to stay for hours, to be treated with a familiarity both kind and flattering, that all his letters repeat the same thing. The dear child tells me about his daily life, and talks to me of those of our friends whom he has met again in Paris, of his amusements, but the invariable conclusion is: 'But the house I like best, which attracts me most, where I always return, is Monsieur Flaubert's.' And there is no danger of my finding this monotonous.

"I cannot say, on the contrary, how happy I am to read those lines . . . to see my son received in this way by the best of our old friends. Am I not, to some extent, responsible for this favour? Does the young man not recall to you a thousand memories of that dear past in which poor Alfred had such a place?

"You said in Rouen that the nephew was like his uncle, and I see, with pardonable maternal pride, that closer examination has not destroyed the illusion. — If you want to make me happy, give me news of yourself. It is good to see that one is not forgotten, to feel that solitude does not isolate one completely, and that it cannot affect real friendship.

"Then you must tell me about my son, tell me whether he has read you some of his verses, and whether you think they show anything more than mere facility.

"You know what confidence I have in you; what you believe, I will believe, and I will take your advice. If you say 'yes,' we will encourage the dear boy in the way which he prefers, but if you say 'no,' we'll put him into the wig-making business . . . or something of the kind. . . . So be frank with your old friend."

For an answer to this appeal Madame de Maupassant had not long to wait:

"My dear Laure: Your letter anticipated mine, for I have been intending for a month to write and tell you how fond I am of your son. You have no idea how charming I find him; intelligent, good-humoured, sensible, and amusing; in short (to employ a fashionable word), how sympathetic. Despite the difference in our ages I regard him as 'a friend' — he reminds me so much of poor Alfred. Sometimes the resemblance frightens me, especially when he lowers his head in reciting poetry. What a man he was! He remains in my memory as beyond all comparison. Every day I think of him. I am afraid I am obsessed by the dead (my dead). Is that a sign of old age? I suppose so.

"When shall we two meet again? When can we talk about this young man? Couldn't you come with the two boys and spend a few days at Croisset? I have plenty of room for you now, and I envy the serenity you seem to enjoy, for I am growing very gloomy. My existence and the present age lie heavily upon my shoulders, horribly. I am so disgusted with every-thing, and especially with the advance guard of litera-ture, that I have stopped publishing. Life is no longer pleasant for people of taste.

"Nevertheless, you must encourage your son in his taste for poetry, because it is a noble passion; literature is a consolation for many misfortunes, and perhaps he may have talent. Who knows? So far he has not produced enough for me to draw his poetic horoscope. Besides, who can decide a man's future?

"I think our young friend is rather dilatory and not very keen on work. I should like to see him do some sustained piece of writing, however bad. What he has shown me is certainly as good as anything the Parnas-sians publish. — With time he will become more origi-nal, acquire a personal way of seeing and feeling (that's the whole secret). As for the results, for success — what do they matter? The chief thing in this world is to keep one's soul aloof, far from the slime of bour-geois democracy. The cult of art engenders pride, of which one can never have too much. That is my morality."

Flaubert's affection for Alfred Le Poittevin's nephew did not deprive him of his judgment, and, while he ad-mitted the possibility of some talent, he aroused no false hopes either in mother or son. The latter appeared to all his friends as a robust young man from the coun-try, with little of the air of a poet about him, more inclined to display his muscular prowess than his intelli-gence, and passionately devoted to rowing. "He had," to quote a friend, "the round ruddy face of a fresh-water sailor, and simple easy manners. We used to think that insomnia, dyspepsia, and certain nervous troubles were part of the dignity of a writer. At this time Maupassant showed no signs of neurasthenia. His skin and com-

plexion were those of a countryman exposed to the open
air, and he spoke with a countrified drawl. He thought
of nothing but walking tours and rowing on Sundays.
He would live nowhere but on the banks of the Seine.
Every day he rose at dawn, washed down his yawl,
rowed a while, and smoked a few pipes. Then he would
take the latest possible train to town, in order to toil and
curse in his official jail. He drank hard, ate heartily,
and slept soundly — and everything else in proportion."

Even these pleasures developed only as his salary
rose to the heights already mentioned. During his
first year or so his resources were extremely limited, as
this memorandom of 1872 shows:

Received for one month's expenses: 110 francs.

Debit.	Francs
Concierge	10
Mending	3.50
Coal	4.00
Firewood	1.90
Firelighters	0.50
Laundry	7.00
Stamps	0.40
30 lunches	36.00
30 dinners	48.00
Haircut	0.60
2 sulphur baths	2.00
Sugar	.40
Coffee	.60
Lamp oil	5.50
Rolls	3.00
Chimney sweep	5.00
Soap	.50
	128.90

The relatively high expenditure for laundry and lamp
oil is characteristic, and the charge for sulphur baths

gives furiously to think. Flaubert's warning, much ex-
purgated, survives: "Your letter amused me hugely,
young man! But, in the interests of literature, I warn
you to go slow." Guy apparently had Uncle Alfred's
gift for realism, which produced such a wealth of aster-
isks when their correspondence was published. The
Rabelaisian sage of Croisset talked to his "adopted
son" in the same vein. « *Vous vous plaignez du c . . .
des femmes qui sont 'monotones.' Il y a un remède bien
simple, c'est de ne pas vous en servir. . . . Il faut, en-
tendez-vous, jeune homme, il faut travailler plus que ça.
J'arrive à vous soupçonner d'être caleux. Trop de p . . . !
Trop de canotage, trop d'exercice.* » Turgenev also noted
that young M. Maupassant's hair was falling out, and
the nature of his amusements, as described in *Mouche*,
will explain why his appearance of robust health was
deceptive. Despite the gay parties on the river, with
Mouche and her like, the strenuous boating, and the
pride in his muscles, which prompted him to singular
forms of exhibitionism, the disciple of Flaubert was a
sick man and a hypochondriac.

"Beware of melancholy, my dear Guy, it is a vice to
which one surrenders, and when the immediate cause
has passed, one's precious strength has been wasted, and
one is exhausted"; but gloomy letters and continual
complaints about his health reached Croisset, provoking
always the same exhortations. "Your health will be
better if you follow your vocation." "You are born to
write poetry. Write! Nothing else matters, especially
your health and your amusements." But "there is an
atmosphere of lubricity in Paris just now which I like
. . . the shamelessness of the dear public is delightful"
— and what advice could prevail against a temperament
so propitiously served?

Madame de Maupassant's health was also a subject

of much concern both to her husband and her son at this time. "Just a line, Mother dear, to tell you of a conversation that took place last night. I had just seen my father, who told me about Dr. Lacronique's visit and what the latter said to him. As I had to see Suzanne Lagier, I went to her house, and there I met Dr. Duplay. I spoke to him about you and described, with as much detail as possible, every symptom of your illness. He replied that he did not see anything indicating serious organic disease, but that steps should at once be taken to check its course, as something might happen which could not afterwards be cured. Sulphate of quinine could afford only temporary relief, but Dr. Lacronique's idea seemed very logical to him, and until proof of the contrary, he would believe that you have a tapeworm. When it is lodged in certain positions, it cannot be expelled, because the coils that break off are digested by the stomach. But that might take a long time — I accepted this theory all the more readily because Hervé had one, and he might have got it from you, assuming you had such a thing for many years.

"In nine cases out of ten no trace of tapeworm can be seen and it takes the form of all sorts of diseases, especially *nervous* diseases of the stomach and *heart*. The symptoms are so varied that the doctors are baffled. . . . The very strangeness of your disease is almost certain proof to the two doctors in question of the existence of a tapeworm whose presence has not yet been discovered. . . ."

This digestible tapeworm has carried no conviction of Maupassant's knowledge of medicine, but it is the only evidence, at this early stage, of a nervous disease in the mother which also affected her younger son, and in the light of the subsequent medical history of all three members of the family, the letter is worth noting. Until her death Laure de Maupassant showed a great aversion to all theories of heredity; she forbade the publication of a thesis on Maupassant's heredity, and when the few letters of his that have been allowed to appear in print are examined, discreet dots occur significantly. Thus, when he wrote to Flaubert on the subject of his mother's health and other worries:

"You ask me for news, but alas, I have only bad news. In the first place, my mother is not at all well. . . . In addition to all that, the office is getting on my nerves; I can't work. My mind is sterile and tired by the figures I add up from morning until night. At times I feel so sharply the futility of everything, the blind cruelty of life, the emptiness of the future (whatever it may be), that I am filled with a melancholy indifference to all things, and I want nothing better than to remain quiet, quietly in a corner, without hopes or troubles.

"I am living all alone, because people bore me, and I bore myself because I cannot work. My thoughts are mediocre and monotonous, and my mind is so stiff that I cannot express them. . . ."

Even then, however, there was one bright spot, and, needless to say, it lay in the direction of all Maupassant's flights from reality!

"From time to time I go to our good friend Mme. Brainne for an hour or two. She is the best woman in the world and I am very fond of her. I tell her a lot of stories which must seem to her, I fancy, rather crude at times. She does not find me very sentimental. She tells me her dreams and I stick to realities.

"To other lovely creatures whom I meet there I whisper the secret pleasures of lubricity, and I lose their affection because I am not sufficiently respectful."

Then again, the complaint is heard:

"I am completely demoralized.   For three weeks I

have tried every night to work without producing a single good page. Absolutely nothing. I am gradually sinking into depths of discouragement from which it will be hard to emerge. The office is killing me little by little. After seven hours of 'administrative labours' I cannot react sufficiently to throw off the weight that harasses my mind. I even tried to send a few articles to *Le Gaulois* in order to make a little money, but I couldn't. I haven't an idea and feel like crying over my paper. To make matters worse, everything is going wrong. Mother, who went back to Étretat two months ago, is not the slightest bit better. Her heart is making her suffer a great deal, and she has had some very distressing fainting fits. She is so weak that she cannot write to me any more. All I get is a line every fortnight which she dictates to the gardener."

At the Ministry of Marine he gets no respite: "My chief, for the sole purpose of being disagreeable to me, no doubt, has just given me the most horrible work in the office, work which was being done quite well by an old stick-in-the-mud . . . figures, figures all the time, and as I am with him, I cannot do any work of my own, even in my leisure moments. That, I think, is his object. Everything is depressing. Mother is very ill and cannot even leave Etretat. . . ."

Upon which Flaubert's characteristic comment is:

"*Vous vivez dans un enfer de m . . .*, I know, and I am very sorry for you. But from 5 p.m. until 10 a.m. you can give can give all your time to the Muse, who is, after all, the best of wenches. Come along, my dear boy, pull yourself together. What is the use of dwelling on your troubles? Be a strong man to yourself, it is the only way to become one. Have some pride, by heaven! Your uncle had more backbone. What you need is 'principles.' Despite what people say, they are neces-

sary — whatever they may be.   There is only one principle for an artist: to sacrifice everything to art.   He
should regard life as a means to an end, nothing more,
and the first person for whom he should not care a damn
is himself.

"What has happened to *La Vénus rustique?*   And the
novel, whose plan was so delightful? "

While this correspondence of complaint and exhorta-
tion was passing between Paris and Croisset, Guy de
Maupassant was by no means the obscure slave of
bureaucratic routine that he appeared to be.   Flaubert's
literary discipline had not permitted him to offer any
major work to the public.   He had, however, introduced
him to his own circle, to the Goncourts, Turgenev, and
Zola; Maupassant was writing occasionally for the
newspapers, and he had begun to make acquaintances
and friends of his own age, Huysmans, Céard, Alexis,
Hennique, and all five of them had acquired the habit of
dining together every Thursday and spending the rest of
evening at Zola's.   Already the sinister rumour was
abroad that these presumptuous young men regarded
themselves as constituting a school of literature, and
when they gave a dinner at Trapp's for Flaubert,
Edmond de Goncourt, and Zola, on the 16th of April,
1877, their audacity was a subject important enough
for newspaper comment.   The menu appropriate to
such an occasion was drawn up by *La République des
Lettres:*

> Potage « purée Bovary »
> Truite saumonnée à la « fille Elisa »
> Poularde truffée à la « Saint Antoine »
> Artichauts au « Cœur Simple »
>   Parfait « naturaliste »
>   Vin de « Coupeau »
> Liqueur de l'« Assommoir »

Maupassant and Paul Alexis were the juniors, so far as published works were concerned, for neither of them had a book to his name until 1879, when each of them became the proud author of a one-act play. Huysmans had paid for the publication of his first volume, *Le Drageoir à Epices*, five years earlier, and three works to his credit, including *Marthe* and *Les Sœurs Vatard*. Under the name of Guy de Valmont, Maupassant had published in obscure places four dreadful stories, to be found now only in the appendices to his collected works. Flaubert was all absorbed in the task of making a poet of him, and *La Main d'écorché*, *Le Donneur d'eau bénite*, *Le Mariage du lieutenant Laré*, and *Coco, Coco, Coco frais*, the only stories published during his 'prentice years, represent the efforts of the pupil to escape the vigilance of the master, who would have recoiled in horror from these jejeune elucubrations.

In 1876 he published an essay on Flaubert in *La République des Lettres* which drew a letter from his grateful subject:

"Thanks for your article, my dear friend; you treat me with filial tenderness; my niece is enthusiastic about your work. She thinks it the best thing ever written about her uncle. I think so, too, but I must not say so. The Talmud is a little excessive, however, I am not so great as all that!"

Catulle Mendès had accepted Maupassant's poems in this paper on Flaubert's recommendation, but an attack on Renan had caused Flaubert to sever his connection with it. He was anxious, therefore, to find another place for his *protégé's* work, and Raoul Duval's *Nation* seemed desirable:

"I have asked Raoul Duval to take you on trial; that is, to get you to write two or three book reviews. He agreed to this, so, as soon as parliament meets, I'll

send you a letter of introduction to him. That is settled.
I was warmly seconded in my recommendation by Mme.
Lapierre. Always the ladies, you rascal! . . .

"If you can suggest some work yourself, that will
save him the trouble of thinking, and it will be quicker.
Nobody has done a history of modern criticism; it is a
good subject. For example, take Planche, Janin, Théo,
etc., only those who are dead, and analyse their ideas,
their theories. . . .

"There is no study, nor even an attempt at one, of
the immense achievement of George Sand. A nice parallel could be drawn between her work and that of
Dumas, the novel of adventure and the novel of ideas.
If you get into the *Nation* I want you to start with something that will attract attention. . . ."

This cheerful news was to prove somewhat deceptive,
as Maupassant complained:

"As soon as I got your letter I went to see M. Raoul
Duval, who received me extremely kindly and said:
'We have no literary critic, as yet. Do me an article at
once on some *new* book. I'll see that it goes in. Then
let me have another in a couple of weeks, and I will ask
the board of managers to complete the staff by appoint-
ing you literary critic. You may be certain I will do all
I can, because you have been warmly recommended by
my best friends, G. Flaubert and the Lapierres!'

"Whereupon I went off delighted, bought the Letters
of Balzac, and prepared my article . . . but in a few
days I heard that the *Nation* publishes signed articles by
M. Filon, the ex-tutor of the Prince Imperial, and one of
his friends tells me that he is to do the literary criticism.
However, I finished my article and took it yesterday to
M. Raoul Duval, and I saw him this morning. He was
as amiable as ever, and complimented me on my essay,
which will be printed at once. But I gathered that I am

not to have the post of literary critic; probably the place has been taken by M. Filon. I think I am going to replace a writer of light special articles, who is not good enough, and I shall have the greatest freedom in the choice of my subjects. In any case, M. Raoul Duval seems fully decided to put me on the staff of the paper. . . ."

After a month or so, Maupassant's troubles were so serious that he unburdened himself at great length to the ever-patient Flaubert, who never seemed tired of soothing the spoiled child, so easily upset by the commonest difficulties and disappointments of the career he had chosen.

"When M. R. Duval asked for some literary articles, he refused to accept long and serious studies like the one I suggested. He told me to make it *amusing*. In order to please him, I gave him my article on Balzac, which is criticism for the use of fashionable ladies and gentlemen, without any trace of literature. He thought it charming and spoke *enthusiastically* about it to Mme. Lapierre, who told me so. Thereupon I wrote a very serious and very literary article on a very big and very grave question, *The Invasion of Eccentricity*, the trick of mediocrities to conceal their lack of originality. The book which served me as a pretext for this article was Jean Richepin's *Les Morts bizarres*. R. Duval objected that this would not interest their readers, that M. Richepin did not deserve the advertisement which always resulted even from an unfriendly article (as if I care a pin about Richepin!!!), etc., etc. Then I took the new edition of Sainte-Beuve's first book on French poetry in the sixteenth century, and I wrote a third article. Raoul Duval seemed to like it, asked me to allow him to break up a few sentences, because *brevity is the soul of journalism*, and announced that it would appear shortly. I am still waiting!!!

"As the M. Noël who is doing the dramatic criticism for the *Nation* writes even worse drivel than Mallarmé, and they really cannot keep him, M. R. Duval asked me to write about some plays. I first took *L'Ami Fritz*, which is assuredly the best play of this year. Daudet, Zola, and Turgenev think so, and, what is sufficient for me, I think so. To-day I learn that M. Duval thought it idiotic, atrocious, and is advising everyone not to see it. Is it his opinion or that of the Bonapartists? I do not know. The fact remains that my article must not have pleased him, although I was very moderate in my praise of the play. I see with my own eyes and judge with my own mind, and I will not say that black is white because someone else thinks so. I am going to write one more trial article for the *Nation* and after that I shall stay quiet. Not only have I spent 25 francs on books and theatre tickets, an expense I need not have incurred, but I have lost fully a month's work, which is much more important. This continual uncertainty irritates me; these irregular articles, all on different subjects, upset me. I don't know where I stand, and with M. Raoul Duval's indecision and his fear of a staff obviously hostile to a newcomer, he can keep me all spring writing trial articles, which get me nowhere and are not paid for. . . .

"I should like to know if I am to replace M. Noël. Otherwise, it is useless for me to spend money and time for nothing. I do not even know which play to choose for a second article, and this belated criticism cannot have any kind of originality. In any case, it is useless to write to M. Duval about me. When you are in town I'll tell you all about that in detail. You can take it from me, no paper will allow me to write really literary articles and say what I think. I read the *Nation* every day. This sheet is fundamentally idiotic, the kingdom of prejudice and conventionality. Anything new, in form or substance, will frighten them. . . ."

Holidays from the detested Ministry did not help to brighten Maupassant's outlook; his health was a constant worry, and Flaubert was recommending doctors in addition to suggesting work. "Women's love is as monotonous as men's wit," wailed the disciple. "I find that life is not varied, that our vices are very commonplace, and that there is a scarcity of well-turned phrases." At the office M. de Maupassant was also the subject of official complaint. His capacities seemed mediocre, and he was not discharging his duties satisfactorily. The days and nights on the Seine, between Asnières and Maisons-Laffitte, while producing an external appearance of robustness, had left a mark which, at this time, was visible only to the professional eyes to whose frequent scrutiny Maupassant submitted. The evenings, too, with Céard, Huysmans, and Hennique were not conducive to repose, for at 17, rue Clauzel, Maupassant was surrounded by lady tenants of the kind most amenable to his own special form of unreason. At the end of the evening it was his practice to invite some of these fair creatures in to see him, at the conclusion of their night's toil, and to prove himself *un client sérieux*. It was in vain that Flaubert said "*trop de putains*," and "*je vous engage à vous modérer*." His muscles were not Maupassant's only source of naïve pride.

Listening to Zola reading chapters from *Nana* was not a very satisfactory distraction for the pessimist, and when he heard that Flaubert would not be in Paris during the winter of 1879, his discontent knew no bounds. "To spend the winter without seeing you does not seem possible; my greatest pleasure in the year is to go and chat with you every Sunday for three or four months." But the Master had not been inactive on Maupassant's behalf, before withdrawing to hibernate at Croisset. His friend Bardoux had become Minister of Public Instruction, owing to a change of government, and Flaubert, who would never solicit or accept official favours for himself, laid siege to the new Minister and succeeded in reading a play of Maupassant's to Bardoux, and some poems to Xavier Charmes, the head of the department. He was convinced that this method would be effective in obtaining a better post for the author:

"Caroline writes me that Bardoux will put Guy on his staff in the very near future; he will find a job for Laporte, and will assuredly decorate Zola on New Year's Day. . . . So I suggest you go at once to Charmes and ask him what you ought to do now; if you should resign, and when you will enter the new department." And in due course, early in 1879, "Guy de Maupassant, third-class clerk, sent in his resignation from the Ministry of Marine, in order to accept a post in the Ministry of Public Instruction," according to the records. Already in January his dissatisfaction emerges: "I think the government is at the end of its tether, and I am afraid I shall be forgotten in the crash. My nominal salary is 1800 francs, but if I get no more than that, it will be very little, especially as I cannot for the life of me understand why they did not take me on sooner. . . . Zola has not been decorated — because of his article in the *Figaro*. . . . Can you believe it? . . .

"My play is being rehearsed at the third Théâtre Français, but I haven't yet had time to see a single rehearsal. I arrive here at 9 and leave at 6.30. You may imagine how little leisure I have. I am getting farther and farther away from my unfortunate novel. I am afraid the umbilical cord has been cut. Nevertheless, I hope the government stays in power, for I want to make a little place for myself here. I think I could, and then

I should be able at last to work quietly. . . . Do leave
Croisset, if only for a fortnight, so that we may have a
talk. . . ."

Promptly the answer came: "Don't be upset, I shall
be in Paris at the end of February (or the middle of
March) and shall remain until the end of May. One
can't always live in solitude, and I need the city for my
reading.

"The story of Zola's cross is pitiable. What stupidity! But is there anything that isn't stupid?

"The end of my novel will surpass in violence
Zola's famous article. At least, I hope so! And they
wouldn't decorate me for it. Seriously, I regret having that star, but what saves me is: I never wear it.
Axioms:

"Honours dishonour,
Position stupefies.
Placard the walls with these."

By the end of January the government had not fallen,
but Flaubert had broken his leg. The disciple is full of
concern. His play is about to be produced and he has
no time to go down to Croisset. He would like an introduction to Théodore Banville. Flaubert pursues his
studies of human inbecility to be enshrined in *Bouvard
et Pécuchet,* and protests against a reissue of *Madame
Bovary.* "I am absolutely sick and tired of that book.
Nothing else that I have done seems to exist," his publisher learns. "I assure you that, if I were not hard up,
I should let it go out of print." Huysmans' gift of *Les
Sœurs Vatard* becomes a further complication. It is
"abominable," but "*Le Chat maigre* of Anatole France
is charming." Maupassant is asked: "What am I to
do with your friend Huysmans? Is he the kind of man
to whom one can speak frankly? His *Sœurs Vatard*
arouses only very moderate enthusiasm in me. As he

seems a decent sort of chap, I don't want to offend him. Yet . . ."

The play which Ballande produced on the 19th of February, 1879, was *Histoire du vieux temps*, one act in verse, upon which the author had been working for several years, making drastic revisions under Flaubert's direction. "I recopied my *Histoire du vieux temps* last night," he wrote in 1876, "making all the changes you indicated. I cut out *five pages* at the *beginning*." Now its production was quite a success. "My play went well; much better than I expected. Lapommeraye, Banville, and Claretie were very kind. . . . Daudet was perfidious. He said: 'M. de M., without knowing it, has resurrected Alphonse Karr's yellow roses. Everyone, I imagine, remembers the subject? Then he analysed the yellow roses (of which I knew nothing) in such a way that there was an absolute resemblance to my play. Whereas, from what I hear, there is a marked difference between the two subjects. He concluded with a few words of praise. — Zola said nothing. I hope he'll talk on Monday. In any case, his *crowd* has thrown me over, not finding me sufficiently naturalistic. Not one of them came to shake hands with me after the *success*. Zola and his wife *applauded loudly* and congratulated me afterwards. . . ."

Flaubert saw evidence here of his pupil's success. "Now they will read your manuscripts. As for the little acts of perfidy, you will get accustomed to that kind of thing. I am not surprised that the Naturalists are leaving you in the lurch. *Oderunt poetas*." By way of compensation, he promised that Mme. Pasca would perform the little play at Princess Mathilde's *salon;* Monsieur de Maupassant was to make his entry into high society.

Even at the Ministry of Public Instruction his posi-

tion was somewhat happier. He soon became secretary
to Xavier Charmes, and amongst his colleagues were
kindred spirits from *La République des Lettres*, Henry
Roujon and Léon Dierx. His chiefs were anxious to
advance Maupassant, but he evaded all work of respon-
sibility. Charmes was a bureaucrat of the old school,
whose special pride it was to send out official documents
and letters that were samples of the best French prose.
His assistant, though an author, refused to help in this
laudable enterprise. "It is the fault of the Ministry of
Marine. As soon as there is the slightest flavour of
official work in anything, the official style overcomes me,
and I cannot escape from it." And so he was allowed to
keep records and to look after the most simple matters
of routine. His bad health was a convenient pretext,
and he absented himself an average of three days a week.
Nevertheless, he wrote to Flaubert:

"My dear Master: I am destined always to be the
slave of officialdom. For a week now I have been want-
ing to write to you, and I could not find half an hour in
which to do it. My relations here with Charmes, my
chief, are very agreeable, and we are almost on an equal
footing. He has had a lovely office assigned to me, but
I am his property. He puts half his work on to me. He
walks around and I write from morning until night; I
am attached to an electric bell, and, in the end, I shall
have no more freedom here than at the Marine. The
people are pleasant and the work is not nearly so dull.
The night of my little play Charmes said: 'Clearly, we
must let you have time for work, and rest assured, you
shall have it!!!!!!' Alas, I am too useful to him and he
takes advantage of it. That is always the way. I
wanted to attract his favourable notice and I have succeeded only too well. . . ."

Zola was writing about the "asininities" of Hugo and

outlining the whole duty of Naturalism, to the disgust
of the Master and his disciple.

"What do you think about Zola?   It seems to me he
must be mad.   Did you read his article on Hugo, his
article on contemporary poets, and his pamphlet, *La République et la littérature?* 'The republic will be Naturalistic or nothing ' — 'I am only a scientist ' (only that
— what modesty!)."   But graver matters arise:

"Madame Pasca (between ourselves) nearly died of
grief when Ricard broke with her, and you may take it
from me, she will not do my play at the Princess Mathilde's.   She can think of nothing but her broken heart.
My God, what silly creatures women are! — The Char-
pentiers have reached the lowest depths of stupidity,
and the wife is even worse than her husband.

"I am awaiting you impatiently.   I am bored and do
not feel well.   My circulation is bad and the *doctors* can
only repeat their eternal phrase: 'Exercise.   What you
need is exercise!'   I have no time for work and this
spoils my temper. . . ."

This epistle charmed the patient recipient of such
complaints: "You poor devil, I pity your not having
any time for work.   As if a good line of verse were not
a hundred thousand times more useful to the instruction
of the public than all the solemn rubbish on which you
are engaged.   It is difficult to force simple ideas into
some skulls.

"Yes.   I read Zola's pamphlet.   It is incredible!
When he gives me a definition of Naturalism, perhaps I
shall be a Naturalist.   But until then: me no understand. . . ."

And with a promise to be in Paris in a couple of weeks,
and an anxious inquiry about the unfortunate author of
Les Sœurs Vatard — "Was Huysmans shocked by my
letter? " — Flaubert returned to his "horrible fellows,"

Bouvard and Pécuchet, nursing his lame leg, his lumbago, his blepharitis, and a boil on his face, with the extraction of one of his remaining molars as an interlude! In spite of all these afflictions, he has time for a new effort on behalf of his adopted son, whom he thus draws to the attention of Mme. Juliette Adam of *La Nouvelle Revue:*

"I take the liberty of sending you by this post a poem which I consider remarkable and a worthy adornment for your review.

"The author, Guy de Maupassant, is employed in the offices of the Ministry of Public Instruction. I believe he has a great literary future, in the first place; and in the second, I love him tenderly because he is the nephew of the closest friend I ever had, whom he resembles very much — by the way, the friend . . . to whom I dedicated *Saint Antoine.* In a word, I should be very grateful if you would print his little poem. The young man in question had a one-act play produced by Ballande last winter, *Histoire du vieux temps*, which was a great success. He is known in the group of the Parnassians. . . ."

Then Maupassant is warned:

"I have just written an enthusiastic letter to Mme. Adam, announcing your manuscript, which should reach her to-morrow evening. I did not mention money. When she receives your poem, we shall see. The Republicans are generally so prudish that I am not very sure of its reception. But I think the Goethesque quality of it will seduce the lady. . . ."

Although Turgenev and other friends joined their recommendations to his, Flaubert was disappointed Evidently the lady was not seduced by *La Vénus rustique*, although her friends used to say that for Juliette Adam, Adam was not the first man. "Here is Mme. Juliette Adam's autograph. It may be useful. That's journalism all over! My God! My God! Déroulède and Leconte de Lisle identified, and Theuriet held up as a model!"

As the year closed a characteristic document issued from the Cabinet du Ministre de l'Instruction Publique, des Cultes et des Beaux Arts:

"I have been greatly rushed lately and again I could not write to you. At last I am installed in a nice office looking on to the gardens, but it looks too nice to last. . . .

"I really have no time. I arrive at nine in the morning and leave at half-past six in the evening. I have two hours for lunch. However, this is only temporary, and I shall be very free, once I get back to regular office work.

"I am treated with the highest consideration. The heads of departments are deferential and the chief clerks adore me. The others look on at me from a respectful distance. My colleagues pose, and I think they consider me too simple.

"On the one hand, what I see is silly, silly, silly; on the other sad, sad, sad. In short, everyone is stupid as stupid can be, here as elsewhere. . . .

"An irritating detail. At the Minister's office we have to come every Sunday until noon. However, I think I shall have time to write. My work will go quickly when I am used to it. It is not difficult."

As the year 1879 drew to its close, Maupassant began to prepare for publication a volume of the best poems written under the tutelage of Flaubert. The latter now felt that the time had come when "Guy de Valmont," *chroniqueur* in *Gil Blas* and *Le Figaro*, and poet in *La République des Lettres*, could emerge as Guy de Maupassant, the new Parnassian. In his greeting for the New Year, he said:

"May 1880 weigh lightly upon you, my beloved disciple. No more heart trouble; good health to your mother; a good subject for a play, and may it be well written and bring you in a hundred thousand francs. My good wishes relative to the genital organs come last, as nature herself will look after that.

"So you are going to publish a *volume!* A volume of verse, of course, but apparently, according to your letter, the Rouen story will be included? You say *our* proofs: Who are *we?*"

The secret of a volume of stories to be published under Zola's ægis had been kept from Flaubert, but when he saw Maupassant's contribution, he pronounced it "a masterpiece." Meanwhile the manuscript of *Des Vers* had been delivered to Charpentier, and Flaubert was impatient to see it published, but he had to content himself with *Nana*, which was the most important event of the moment at the Maison Charpentier. "I am flabbergasted by it," Flaubert wrote to Zola, in a letter sprinkled with adjectives of delight: "marvellous," "ineffable beauty," "epic," "sublime." But to Maupassant: "Charpentier must be mad. He is stupid not to have brought out your book long ago." However, when he opened *L'Evènement* of February 13th, 1880, Flaubert discovered that "Monsieur Guy de Maupassant was about to be prosecuted for publishing obscene poetry." *L'Abeille*, the local paper of Etampes, had reprinted a poem from a Parisian periodical, and as this piece was part of the volume in Charpentier's hands, the latter doubtless felt that a little delay would not do any harm. "My disciple, Guy, prosecuted for immorality by *the bench at Etampes!!!*" Flaubert thundered. "What does that mean? Do you know the young man is developing prodigiously? *Boule de Suif* is a jewel, and a week ago he showed me a poem which a master would be proud to sign. *Do* print his book at once, so that it may appear this spring. He is dying to be published and publication will *help* him." With rumours of the possible suppression of *Nana* afloat, however, Charpentier does not seem to have been unduly moved by the appeal.

Maupassant himself was not in any more heroic a mood. Instead of viewing the prosecution as a colossal advertisement for his forthcoming book, his concern is lest he should lose his position. "If I did not fear the prudishness of the Ministry," Flaubert wrote, "I should be delighted," but "we must use all possible influence to have the case quashed." Whereupon he draws up the defence strategically: senators, editors, men and women of letters, and people of importance in the social and political worlds are called upon. By special request Flaubert drew up an open letter to be published in *Le Gaulois:*

"Is it really true? At first I thought it was a joke! But no, I see I was mistaken. What charming creatures they must be in Etampes! Are we to be responsible to every tribunal on French soil, including the colonies! How can they proceed against a poem which has already appeared in a now defunct Parisian paper, and which is reprinted in a provincial sheet which may never have obtained your permission, and whose existence was probably unknown to you? What are we reduced to now? What may we write? How can we publish? In what Bœotia are we living?

"Accused of 'an outrage on morals and public decency,' two pleasant synonyms, which are the two counts in the indictment. I had a third outrage to my credit, 'on religious morals,' when I appeared before the Eighth Chamber with *Madame Bovary.* That trial gave me a gigantic advertisement, to which I attribute three quarters of my success. . . .

"They will say that your poem is obscene in tendency. On the tendency theory a sheep could be executed for having dreamed of mutton. There should be some defi-nite agreement on this question of morality in the State. Whatever is beautiful is moral — that is all there is to be said about it. . . .

"But think of the subject, Mrs. Grundy will say; the subject! Two lovers. A washerwoman! The bank of a river. You should have adopted a light tone, treated the subjects more delicately, finely, insinuated neatly a reproof, and brought in at the end a venerable priest, or a good kind doctor, to deliver a lecture on the dangers of love. In short, your story is an encouragement to the conjunction of the sexes. Ah, ha! . . ."

Having recently declared to Mme. Roger des Ge-nettes, à propos of Père Hyacinthe Loÿson: "The im-portance attached to the sexual act seems very funny to me," Flaubert denies that the poem encourages such enterprises, but points out that the lovers are not guilty of adultery and are therefore, blameless. After the in-evitable citation of equally "immoral" classics that are unmolested, comes a characteristic protest: "Those who write well have two enemies against them: (1) the public, because style makes them think, forces them to work; (2) the government, because they realize we are a power and authorities never like authority in others." Then the peroration:

"The poet is ascending Olympus, his face illuminated by heavenly rays, his heart full of hope, aspiring towards the beautiful, the divine, half-lost in the clear sky — when the heavy paw of the catchpoll thrusts him back into the gutter. His conversation with the Muse is mistaken for the talk of those who corrupt little girls! Perfumed by the waves of Permessus, he is taken for one of those perverts who find their pleasure in haunting urinals. . . ."

Maupassant, however, was troubled not only by the thought of losing his job, but also by his own private opinion of *Au bord de l'eau,* as expressed to Robert Pinchon in 1876, when that poem first appeared in *La République des Lettres:*

"I have written a poem which will at once earn me the reputation of being a great poet. It will appear on the 20th of this month in *La République des Lettres,* provided the owner and publisher does not read it, for this man is a rabid Catholic, and my poem, though chaste in expression, is as immoral and immodest in its theme and images as it could possibly be. Flaubert, full of enthusiasm, told me to send it to Catulle Mendès, the editor of this review, and the latter, who was completely bowled over, is trying to get it in despite the owner. He read it to several of the Parnassians, and last Saturday it was read at a literary dinner where Zola was a guest. It seems I was the subject of conversation for an hour amongst a lot of men who do not know me at all. Zola listened but said nothing. Mendès introduced me to some of the Parnassians, who overwhelmed me with compliments. Nevertheless, it is going rather far to publish the story of two young people who die of too much —! I wonder if I shall not be hauled into court, like the illustrious Barbey d'Aurevilly."

Although the poem, with a wealth of complaisant detail and that note of hungry eroticism which runs through almost all his verse of the period, was a glorification of the amorous self-immolation of a washerwoman and her unusually gifted friend, on the bank of the stream where he first perceived her charms — evoked in no uncertain terms — Maupassant was never tried. *Le Mur,* another poem, which was the specific cause of the prosecution at Etampes, although not mentioned by either Flaubert or the author in reviewing the whole affair, was mild in comparison. Yet, on its appearance

in *La Revue moderne et naturaliste,* the long passage was
omitted in which the shadows of a man and a woman are
thrown upon a wall by the moonlight, revealing in grotesque exaggeration the nature of their activity. *L'A-
beille* had obligingly printed the suppressed portion for
the edification of the citizens of Etampes, thus precipi-
tating the judicial storm from which Maupassant was
saved only by a vast amount of wire-pulling.

Although Maupassant had the lowest opinion of
Mme. Charpentier's intelligence, it was through her that
Flaubert had sought to interest Charpentier in the
young author's poems: "I ask your husband, as a *personal favour,* to publish now, that is, before the month of
April, Guy de Maupassant's volume of verse. . . . I
insist. This Maupassant has a great, great deal of talent.
I tell you so, and I think I know what I am talking
about. His poems are not tiresome . . . nothing
about stars and little birds. In short, *he is my disciple,*
and I love him as I should my own son . . ."

While consoling Maupassant with news of such efforts, Flaubert saw another little one-act play appear, of
which he approved. *Une répétition* was included by
Tresse and Stock, who had published *Histoire du vieux
temps* the year before, in a volume of *Saynètes et Mono-
logues,* of which Flaubert wrote: "Why don't you send
this book to Princess Mathilde, with your card attached
to the title page? I should like to see that play, performed in her drawing-room." It was not produced,
however, during the author's lifetime, and had to wait
until 1904, when his old friend Pinchon arranged it
for its performance at Rouen. Two one-act plays
published, and still no book! Flaubert insists that
Charpentier must make haste, as if the Master had some
premonition that after April he would have little time
to enjoy his pupil's triumph.

As usual, however, it is not of his own health but of Maupassant's that there is much talk. Daudet, Edmond de Goncourt, Zola, and Charpentier are invited down to Croisset on Easter Sunday. "If your eye is all right, see these gents, and find out what time they will arrive. . . . So many foolish and improbable things have occurred to me about your illness that I should like, solely for my own satisfaction, to have you examined by *my* doctor, Fortin, who is only a medical officer, but I have the highest opinion of him. Further, if you have no money for the journey, I have a superb double louis at your disposal. To refuse out of politeness would be caddish on your part . . ."

Les Soirées de Médan had reached Flaubert at last. "*Boule de Suif* dominates the book, which has a stupid title. . . . Hennique has spoiled a fine subject. . . . Céard talks of something about which he knows nothing: the corruption of the Empire." He reread the story and maintained that it was a masterpiece. "Try to write twelve like that and you will be someone." And on Easter Sunday Maupassant was at the station to meet Daudet, Zola, Goncourt, and their publisher. Flaubert, in his "Calabrian hat and short coat, with his large backside in his wrinkled trousers," received them, as Goncourt notes, with an affectionate smile. "The dinner was excellent, a cream sauce with the turbot, which is marvellous. A great deal of wine of all kinds was drunk, and the evening was spent in telling Rabelaisian tales, which made Flaubert burst into that *spluttering* laughter of childhood." Fortin was present, "as it is my intention to make you all drunk and he can 'lavish his skill on the casualties,' " but Maupassant is given a separate room, so that the doctor can attend to him undisturbed, despite the fact that Flaubert had "only four beds available." He had that dilation of the pupil of one eye which shortly afterwards left Dr. Landolt in no doubt as to "the functional disorders accompanying it and the pitiful end that was in store" for the victim.

In April, 1880, *Des Vers* followed on the heels of *Les Soirées de Médan*, and was dedicated "To Gustave Flaubert, the illustrious and fraternal friend whom I love with all tenderness, to the irreproachable master whom I admire above all." It touched the great heart: "You are right to love me, for your old friend cherishes you. I read the volume at once, knowing three quarters of it already. We shall go over it again together. What I like best is that it is your own. No affectations, no poses! Neither Parnassian nor Realistic (Impressionistic or Naturalistic). Your dedication disturbed in me a whole world of memories! Your uncle Alfred, your grandmother, your mother, and for a while the old man's heart was heavy and his eyes were filled with tears. Collect for me everything that appears on *Boule de Suif* and your book of poems."

Guy de Maupassant was now launched. In a couple of weeks *Les Soirées de Médan* had gone into eight editions. Flaubert drummed up supporters in the press. "I have done what you ask. My letter for Banville will be in Paris to-night. Next week bring me a list of the idiots who write the so-called literary articles in the papers. Then we'll line up our batteries." *Boule de Suif* and *Après la bataille* were the only stories in the volume that had never been published before, but the former received most of the attention. The author, however, was not willing to take any chances. His escape at Etampes had been a narrow one, and his colleagues at the Ministry noticed a very different Maupassant from the burly, boisterous, challenging figure, boasting of his strength, and shocking the bourgeoisie

Guy de Maupassant at the age of ten

Madame Laure de Maupassant and her niece, about 1889. This photograph, taken by Maupassant himself, is the only one of his mother in existence.

by his language at Asnières and Sartrouville, under the benevolent eye of Maman Levanneur. He was "correct, deferential, and discreet, so discreet and frightened that he was afraid to resign when he decided to take his freedom."

When the fatal moment came, he made an appeal to the kindness of Xavier Charmes, who had published a forgotten book of poems in his day, and always considered Maupassant, contrary to the latter's complaints. "My health is bad and the profession of letters is hazardous. If illness or bad luck compelled me, I should like to return to my post and my salary." So he was placed *en disponibilité*, and would have remained so indefinitely, had not some inquisitive bureaucrat decided that the situation had lasted too long. Charmes had to notify Maupassant, who only then resigned, and with great reluctance. He was more typically Norman in his caution and shrewdness about money matters than his Master. When Flaubert received a thousand francs for his *Trois Contes* from *Le Moniteur*, he inquired naïvely: "So literature pays, does it?" His friends had infinite trouble in persuading him to accept a pension of 3000 francs from the government, after he had given all his fortune to his nephew to save the latter from financial ruin. An imaginary post as "unattached" librarian to the Mazarin Library was invented, with the connivance of Jules Ferry, in order to spare him the humiliation of charity.

Flaubert's last letter to Maupassant closes their correspondence as it began, with anxiety as to his physical welfare and untired efforts to promote his literary success:

"(1) I have just sent your address to Mme. Adam, because I cannot read her secretary's signature. Here is the letter; now be off to the *Nouvelle Revue*.

"(2) Have you been to Princess Mathilde's?

"(3) Tell Charpentier to send me two copies of *Les Soirées de Médan*, one for lending purposes and one to give away, in addition to my own copy, which I hope to receive to-morrow. . . .

"I have received a lovely letter from your dear mother.

"Is your eye making you suffer? In a week Bouchet will be here and he will give me details about your illness, which is quite beyond my comprehension." Fortin has refrained from expressing his opinion, but Flaubert's surmise to his niece was not far wrong. "Guy is suffering a great deal. He went to bed to-night at nine o'clock. He has probably the same nervous disease as his mother " — at which point his reflections were censored before publication.

An autograph presentation copy from all six authors of *Les Soirées de Médan* duly arrived, and Mme. Brainne revised her opinion as to the immorality of *Boule de Suif*, receiving in 1883, as her reward, the dedication of *Une Vie* "in memory of a dead friend." Young M. Jules Lemaître, who was recommended to Maupassant's protection, although he never believed that Flaubert's *protégé* had any literary ability, until after the event, called to say good-bye on his way to Algiers as professor of literature.

On the 27th of April, the feast of Saint-Polycarpe was the last treat of Flaubert's life. "The Lapierres surpassed themselves! I received nearly 30 letters from different parts of the world, and three telegrams, while at dinner. The Archbishop of Rouen, Italian cardinals, scavengers, the corporation of floor polishers, a dealer in holy pictures, and others presented their homages to me.

"As presents I received a pair of silk socks, a muffler,

three bouquets, a laurel wreath, a portrait (Spanish) of Saint Polycarpe, a tooth (the relic of a saint), and a box of flowers is coming from Nice. An orchestra that was ordered failed to put in an appearance.

"Letters from Raoul Duval and his two daughters. Verses from young Brainne. All the letters (including Madame Régnier's) had a picture of my patron saint as a heading.

"I was nearly forgetting a menu composed of dishes named after my works. I was really *touched* by all the trouble taken to amuse me. I suspect my disciple of having had a large share in these agreeable pleasantries. . . ."

Finally, Guy gave him the botanical information which had led to such disputes with Baudry, and which was necessary, amongst other strange detail, to the completion of *Bouvard and Pécuchet*. He worked early and late on the first volume, unable to sleep in the fever of composition. On the 2nd of May, 1880, he believed he would reach the second last scene by the following Saturday. Then he would see Charpentier and ask for his accounts, and give Émile Bergerat a piece of his mind for maltreating his work in *La Revue Moderne*, where a fairy-tale, *Le Château des Cœurs*, was running serially. On Saturday, however, Bergerat published the final instalment, but Flaubert did not appear.

With his bag all packed he was preparing for the journey, when he was seized by a stroke of apoplexy. This time the ether he inhaled failed to bring him round. He stumbled to the sofa, lay there breathing stertorously, and soon expired. He was "tired to the very marrow of his bones," as he said, and there was not a minute to be lost over the work dearest to his heart, his retort to the malice, cruelty, and stupidity of life, *Bouvard et Pécuchet*. But that was not to be. He lived just long enough to see the first fruits of the apprentice-ship which he so wisely made Maupassant serve. For ten years he kept his disciple in the background, teaching him his business, little knowing that the years of achievement were to be scarcely longer than those of preparation. Nor could he foresee that nothing in this achievement would ever surpass, and much more would rarely equal, the story whose fame was Flaubert's own final literary success, a joy which was with him to the last moment of his existence.

CHAPTER III

APPRENTICESHIP

THE relation of Flaubert to Maupassant was much more than that of a consoler and older family friend. They were master and pupil in as literal a sense of those terms as is compatible with any originality in the younger man. If Flaubert's first answer to the anxious mother's inquiry as to her son's prospects was a refusal to draw his "poetic horoscope," he was soon unable to maintain so detached an attitude towards Alfred Le Poittevin's nephew, who early discovered the way into the great man's affections. "Dear Sir and Friend," Maupassant wrote in the earliest letter, "our weekly talks have become a habit and a necessity for me, and I cannot resist the desire to chat again by letter. Of course, I do not expect you to reply, I know you have other things to do. Pardon this liberty, but when talking with you I often felt as if I could hear my uncle, whom I did not know, but of whom you and my mother have spoken so often, and whom I love as if I had been his friend or his son, and also poor Bouilhet, whom I did know and also liked very much. I can almost see your gatherings at Rouen, and I regret not to have been one of them, instead of being with boys of my age, who have no idea of what exists."

Soon Laure was assuring Gustave that the disciple belonged to his master, and the latter introduced the young poet and playwright to his own circle, confident that they would some day hear more of Guy de Maupassant. He had no prose stories upon which to found his judgment, for "Guy de Valmont" presented himself almost exclusively as a writer of verse and poetic plays. In 1873 Laure de Maupassant received from her son "something in the style of *Contes du Lundi*," which Daudet had just published, with a request for its return in case he should use it. Whether it was one of the four sketches which adorned the *Almanach de Pont-à-Mousson* in 1875, or *La Mosaïque* in 1876 and 1877, no word of these efforts reached Croisset. On the other hand, in 1874, already *Histoire du vieux temps* was written and submitted to Flaubert for revision, but only the author's mother heard of the "boating scenes" on which he was also working. On the 8th of March, 1875, however, Maupassant was engaged upon his first play to be produced, and this was neither poetic nor a secret from Flaubert. "Some friends and I are going to produce in Leloir's studio an *absolutely lubricious* play, to which Flaubert and Turgenev are coming."

This unexpected first offering was *La Maison turque à la feuille de Rose*, and unlike the author's other *erotica*, it has never been printed. It related the initiation of a bride who is taken straight from the ceremony to a brothel, and it has been described as a dramatization of the *Kama Sutra*. It pleased the spectators so hugely that two years later Flaubert was anxiously asking, "What has happened to *La feuille de Rose*? When do we see it?" In response to repeated demands — some feminine — it was decided to give a second performance at Becker's studio, as Maupassant wrote to Pinchon at Rouen. "We have a very fine studio for our play, belonging to a painter whose name I have forgotten. Eight masked women will be present on this occasion. Immediately after Easter send me the manuscript by post, so that I may have the parts copied. Your arrival seems to me rather late. As Flaubert is leaving Paris early, the piece must be played before the 3rd of May."

Again the play was a colossal success with its selected public, although the plump Suzanne Lagier's pruderies were outraged and she left the room. Turgenev applauded, Zola remained serious, and Flaubert enthusiastically declared that this violent love adventure was "refreshing," the principal part being played, in a blue frock coat with gold buttons, by one of the most distinguished members of the Goncourt Academy. Nevertheless, despite the approval of Edmond de Goncourt, Turgenev, Zola, Meilhac, and Henry Céard, who were among the happy spectators at one or both performances, and notwithstanding the collaboration of "three odalisques" favourably known to connoisseurs at Étretat, Maupassant was threatened with proceedings by the authorities, which added to his nervousness when the case of *Des Vers* for the second time imperilled his existence as a respectable Civil Servant.

At this time, however, Maupassant had more serious preoccupations. "I am working at my novel just now. It is terribly difficult, especially the fitting of each thing into its place and the transitions. However, I shall be well advanced in four or five months. . . ." A year later Flaubert was asking what had become of this novel, the plan of which delighted him, but apparently it was abandoned for ever, unlike that strange novelette, *Le Docteur Héraclius Gloss*, which emerged in 1920, but belongs to the earliest period of his prose writings. "I am absolutely at a loss to know how to arrange the chapter of the servant girl and the monkey in *Héraclius*, and I am in a bad fix. I am beginning my comedy *Une Répétition*, and as soon as it is finished, I shall write, as well as my series of boating stories, a series called *Grandes Misères des petites gens*. I have six already which I consider very good. But they are certainly not amusing." But soon Robert Pinchon heard of his discouragement: "For the moment I am not interested in the theatre. The producers are really not worth working for! It is true they find our plays charming, but they will not put them on. I should prefer them to think the plays bad but to produce them. In other words, Raymond Deslandes thinks my *Répétition* too delicate for the audiences at the Vaudeville."

Of all these projects Flaubert heard only of *Une Répétition*, and that not until five years later. "First let us speak of *Répétition*, then we can talk about *Boule de Suif*. Well, it is very nice, very nice! The part of René would make any actor's reputation, and it is full of good lines, such as the last on page 53. I shall not pick out any others, as I am in a hurry. The lover's *volte-face* and the arrival of the husband are dramatic." He had seen *La Comtesse de Béthune* in 1876, an historical drama, the most elaborate work for the theatre attempted by Maupassant, but in 1878 the latter wrote to Pinchon: "I have wasted nearly the whole winter rewriting my play, but it does not please me," and he swore he would never try the theatre again. Pinchon showed this drama to Ballande, who liked it but wanted something less costly to produce. Whereupon, with Flaubert at his elbow, Maupassant wrote *Histoire du vieux temps*, and abandoned for many years all thought of writing for the stage.

Poetry seemed at this time to be his real talent, and Flaubert declared that even his earliest work, which was excluded from *Des Vers*, "was just as good as anything the Parnassians printed." Upon the selection and polishing of what was to go into that volume both master and disciple concentrated. Jules Lemaître, in 1876, heard Flaubert declaiming *Au bord de l'eau*, when he

first visited Croisset with Maupassant, but Henry Roujon admitted that Catulle Mendès gazed dubiously at
the manuscript when Flaubert recommended it for publication in *La République des Lettres*. Finally, the poem
appeared, between a play by Léon Dierx and a fragment
by Edgar Allan Poe. "Some Parnassians, who never
trifled with questions of technique, raised objections,
but it was generally agreed that the author was 'someone.'"

Maupassant assuredly exaggerated his own daring in
boasting of the poem to Robert Pinchon, but he was
crudely accurate in his summary of the theme: death
through amorous excess. Characteristic of the exacer-
bated note of sensuality which pervaded his verse is
this picture of the woman who excites the man's desire
as she washes clothes in the river:

> Elle choisit sa place, et dans un baquet d'eau,
> D'un geste souple et fort abattit son fardeau.
> Elle avait tout au plus la toilette permise;
> Elle lavait son linge; et chaque mouvement
> Des bras et de la hanche accusait nettement,
> Sous le jupon collant et la mince chemise,
> Les rondeurs de la croupe et les rondeurs des seins.
> Elle travaillait dur; puis, quand elle était lasse,
> Elle élevait les bras, et, superbe de grâce,
> Tendait son corps flexible en renversant ses reins.
> Mais le puissant soleil faisait craquer les planches;
> Le bateau s'entr'ouvrait comme pour respirer.
> Les femmes haletaient; on voyait sous leurs manches
> La moiteur de leur bras par place transpirer.
> Une rougeur montait à sa gorge sanguine.
> Elle fixa sur moi son regard effronté,
> Dégrafa sa chemise, et sa ronde poitrine
> Surgit, double et luisante, en pleine liberté,
> Ecartée aux sommets et d'une ampleur solide.
> Elle battait alors son linge, et chaque coup

Agitait par moment d'un soubresaut rapide
Les rose fleurs de chair qui se dressent au bout.

For five whole months, every night, on the river's
bank

Plein d'un emportement qui jamais ne faiblit,
J'ai caressé sur l'herbe ainsi que dans un lit
Cette fille superbe, ignorante et lascive.

and the nights seemed long in coming around, although
their days were filled with the greedy contemplation of
each other, and of such phenomena in nature as seemed
to give the encouragement of example to their mortal
madness.   They realize that "the love which means
death" possesses them, but, "drunk with old ecstasies,"
they are drawn, in spite of themselves, to the scene of
their joys:

Depuis lors, envahis par une fièvre étrange,
Nous hâtons sans répit cet amour qui nous mange.
Bien que la mort nous gagne, un besoin plus puissant
Nous travaille et nous force à mêler notre sang.
Nos ardeurs ne sont point prudentes ni peureuses;
L'effroi ne trouble pas nos regards embrasés;
Nous mourons l'un par l'autre, et nos poitrines creuses
Changent nos jours futurs comme autant de baisers.
Nous ne parlons jamais.   Auprès de cette femme
Il n'est qu'un cri d'amour, celui du cerf qui brame.
Ma peau garde sans fin le frisson de sa peau
Qui m'emplit d'un désir toujours âpre et nouveau,
Et si ma bouche a soif, ce n'est que de sa bouche!
Mon ardeur s'exaspère et ma force s'abat
Dans cet accouplement mortel comme dans un combat,

Until one day the two bodies are found on the river's
bank, and the people say:

Voilà le mort d'amour avec sa lavandière.

Au bord de l'eau fairly represents a volume overflowing with physical images and desires, written out of a mood of intense excitement, and filled with "furious desires," "savage kisses," "mad desires," and "burning thrills." Even in *La Vénus rustique,* the longest and most serious of the poems, the attempted pantheism, the effort to identify Love with the Beautiful, are largely obscured by the sheer sensuality of the poet's imagination. In his rustic Venus Maupassant saw chiefly what he always saw in the female of the species:

> Le doux effort des seins en sa robe enfermés
> Gonflait l'étoffe, usant aux sommets son corsage.

The men of the countryside would die for her favours, and

> Elle riait, sentant l'ardeur de leurs prunelles,
> Puis passait son chemin, tranquille, et soulevant,
> Au vent de ses jupons, les passions charnelles.

And when a crowd of them fight for her:

> Alors ce fut, dans l'ombre, une opaque mêlée,
> Un tas d'hommes en rut luttant, comme des cerfs
> Lorsque la blonde biche a fait bramer les mâles.

She contemplates the "ferocious struggle" with "eyes full of pride," and she gives herself to the strongest:

> Il s'élança vers elle, ivre et couvert de sang;
> Et sous l'arbre touffu qui leur servait d'alcôve
> Elle reçut sans peur ses caresses de fauve!

The washerwoman and her admirer are not far from the poet's mind:

> Elle s'abandonnait sans resistance, née
> Pour cette œuvre charnelle, et le jour ou la nuit,

> Sans jamais un soupir de bonheur ou d'ennui,
> Acceptant leurs baisers comme une destinée.

Even

> Les animaux aussi l'aimaient étrangement.
> Elle avait avec eux des caresses humaines,
> Et près d'elle ils prenaient des allures d'amant.

Flaubert found *La Vénus rustique* "very good." "All I can see to criticise in it are a few slight grammatical weaknesses, and even they can be defended. You may rest easy. It is good." But *Désirs*, which is a variation on Maupassant's usual theme — not to say obsession — met with harsher criticism. "Well, young man, this poem does not please me at all. It betrays deplorable facility. *Un de mes chers désirs* — a desire that is dear! *Avoir des ailes*, that is indeed a common wish! The next two lines are good, but in the fourth the *oiseaux surpris* are not surprised since you are trying to catch them. Does 'surprised' mean 'astonished'? *Je voudrais, je voudrais.* With such phrases you can go on indefinitely, so long as the ink lasts! And where is your construction? *Ainsi qu'un grand flambeau* — the image seems funny to me: besides, a torch does not leave a flame but carries it.

Des fronts en cheveux noirs aux fronts en cheveux roux. Very nice, but is too much an echo of Ménard's

Sous tes cheveux châtains et sous tes cheveux gris. 'Oui, je voudrais.' Why *Oui?*

Clair de lune — excellent

L'affolante bataille — atrocious!

In short, I suggest that you suppress this piece. It is not up to the level of the others."

The pupil heeded this harsh criticism to the extent of making certain changes, but the poem went into the volume, where it now impresses one, not as being so

very different from the other poems, but as a succinct
expression of Maupassant's philosophy of life:

Le rêve pour les uns serait d'avoir des ailes,
De monter dans l'espace en poussant de grands cris,
De prendre entre leurs doigts les souples hirondelles,
Et de se perdre, au soir, dans les cieux assombris.

D'autres voudraient pouvoir écraser des poitrines
En renfermant dessus leurs deux bras écartés;
Et, sans ployer des reins, les prenant aux narines,
Arrêter d'un seul coup les chevaux emportés.

Moi, ce que j'aimerais, c'est la beauté charnelle:
Je voudrais être beau comme les anciens dieux,
Et qu'il restât aux cœurs une flamme éternelle
Au lointain souvenir de mon corps radieux.

Je voudrais que pour moi nulle ne restât sage,
Choisir l'une aujourd'hui, prendre l'autre demain;
Car j'aimerais cueillir l'amour sur mon passage,
Comme on cueille des fruits en étendant la main.

Ils ont, en y mordant, des saveurs différentes;
Ces aromes divers nous les rendent plus doux.
J'aimerais promener mes caresses errantes
Des fronts en cheveux noirs aux fronts en cheveux roux.

J'adorerais surtout les rencontres des rues,
Les ardeurs de la chair que déchaîne un regard,
Les conquêtes d'une heure aussitôt disparues,
Les baisers échangés au seul gré du hasard.

Je voudrais au matin voir s'éveiller la brune
Qui vous tient étranglé dans l'étau de ses bras;
Et, le soir, écouter le mot que dit tout bas
La blonde dont le front s'argente au clair de lune.

Puis, sans un trouble au cœur, sans un regret mordant,
Partir d'un pied léger vers une autre chimère.
— Il faut dans ces fruits-là ne mettre que la dent:
On trouverait au fond une saveur amère.

Maupassant's obsession is more than the normal pre-occupation of a passionate adolescent. He was a man of thirty years when he published this book of verse, in which even a couple of grandparents are described, in *La dernière escapade*, as dying from the sexual excitement of revisiting the scene of their youthful love. Twelve poems out of a total of nineteen — and those the most important — have but one theme, which is treated in such a manner as to suggest satyriasis rather than the healthy lusts or the sentimental passion of a young poet. When Maupassant was not frenzied by desire, another hallucination seems, even at this early date, to have visited him, as if to indicate a certain sequence of events, in which *Des Vers* foreshadows his own life.

Ce soir-là j'avais lu fort longtemps quelque auteur,
Il était bien minuit, et tout à coup j'eus peur,
Peur de quoi? je ne sais, mais une peur horrible.
Je compris, haletant et frissonnant d'éffroi,
Qu'il allait se passer une chose terrible...
Alors il me sembla sentir derrière moi
Quelqu'un qui se tenait debout, dont la figure
Riait d'un rire atroce, immobile et nerveux:
Et je n'entendais rien, cependant. O torture!
Sentir qu'il baissait à toucher mes cheveux,
Et qu'il allait poser sa tête sur mon épaule,
Et que j'allais mourir au bruit de sa parole!...
Il se penchait toujours vers moi, toujours plus près;
Et moi, pour mon salut eternel, je n'aurais
Ni fait un mouvement ni détourné la tête...
Ainsi que des oiseaux battus par la tempête;
Mes pensers tournoyaient comme affolés d'horreur.
Une sueur de mort me glaçait chaque membre

Et je n'entendais pas d'autre bruit dans ma chambre
Que celui de mes dents qui claquaient de terreur.

Un craquement se fit soudain; fou d'épouvante,
Ayant poussé le plus terrible hurlement
Qui soit jamais sorti de poitrine vivante,
Je tombais sur le dos, roide et sans mouvement.

In that carefully censored correspondence of theirs no
record will be found of any allusion to this either by
Maupassant or by Flaubert. The "good giant" of
Croisset may not have been impressed by it, for its significance is not poetical but pathological, and he could
not know that this terror was to become more and more
frequent, to be recorded in various stories, which psy-
chiatrists subsequently studied to their advantage, until
finally only the professional ears of Dr. Blanche and his
colleagues at Passy could hear what hallucinations destroyed the mind of Guy de Maupassant. Because of
the same censorship, no edition of his works contains a
poem of his early twenties, which also indicates that the
romance of the streets

Les ardeurs de la chair que déchaîne un regard
Les conquêtes d'une heure aussitôt disparues
Les baisers échangés au seul gré du hasard

induced less agreeable consequences and reflections than
are recorded in *Désirs*.

Sa joue etait gluante et suait sous le fard,
Son œil glauque s'ouvrait stupide et sans regard,
Sa mamelle ballait et tombait sur son ventre,
Sa mâchoire édentée et noire comme un antre,
Hideuse s'entrouvrait, foyer d'infections
Qui vous sautaient au nez avec chaque parole,
On sentait clapoter sous la chair flasque et molle
Le liquide visqueux des putréfactions.

In his hours of optimistic tumescence Maupassant could develop the theme of

> Un joli pied cambré qui trottine et qui fuit,
> Un bout de jupon blanc qui passe et se trémousse.

And even when his conquest turns out to be a boating girl — those famous *canotières* of his — the poet finds her an excellent substitute for the lady of his dreams. As *Une Conquête* says:

> Quand on n'a pas de grive, il faut manger un merle.

Maupassant began early to accept "blackbirds" instead of "quail" and preserved throughout his lifetime a remarkable taste for both. Flaubert's admonitions on this subject were not heeded so readily as his advice upon literary matters, for Maupassant was a more docile pupil than Louis Colet, who disputed the judgment of both Flaubert and Bouilhet.

Even *Boule de Suif* did not escape correction: "I am anxious to tell you that I consider *Boule de Suif* a masterpiece. Yes, young man. Nothing more nor less. It is the work of a master: very original in conception, thoroughly realized, and excellent in style. The setting and characters are vivid, and the psychology is powerful. In brief, I am delighted. Two or three times I laughed aloud. That Mme. Brainne should be shocked astounds me. Am I dreaming?! . . .

"On a slip of paper your old pedagogue has put a few comments. Consider them carefully, I think they are sound.

"This little story will *live*, you may be sure of that! What lovely creatures your bourgeois are! You have not missed one. Cornudet is fine and real! The nun pitted with smallpox — perfect, and the count — 'my dear child' — and the ending! The poor girl crying while he sings the *Marseillaise* — sublime. I could kiss you for it! No, really! I am pleased! It amused me and I admire it.

"Now, just because the subject is daring and will irritate the bourgeoisie, I would take out two things, which are all right, but might make some idiot protest, because they seem to imply: 'I don't care a damn!' 'Dans quelle fosse, etc.' — the young man is dragging the army in the mud; (2) the word *tétons*. Aside from these the most prudish taste can find no fault with you.

"Your whore is charming! If you could reduce her belly at the beginning, you would do me a favour."

The first phrase was completely eliminated from the passage describing the panic on the approach of the Prussians, when the national guards hide their arms and uniforms. The word *tétons* occurred in the description of Boule de Suif's adipose tissue: "*Il aperçut Boule de Suif, dont le ventre et les tétons se mêlaient sous un peignoir de cachemire bleu.*" The decorous substitute was: "*Boule de Suif, qui paraîssait plus replète encore,*" and "*un gros bedon qui saillait sous sa robe*" became "*une gorge énorme,*" in response to Flaubert's concluding request. The latter was determined that the scandal caused by the second performance of *La Maison turque* should not be repeated, but he had "certain ideas as to how to make *Boule de Suif* known." It was to be Zola, however, who actually did the propaganda for *Les Soirées de Médan,* and to him Flaubert had warmly recommended the story, when Maupassant first showed it to him in manuscript.

In the years of his apprenticeship Maupassant appeared to Zola little more than a youth fresh from college who used to be seen every Sunday at Flaubert's apartment looking out on to the trees of the Parc Monceau. "As soon as we arrived he would modestly take a back seat, rarely speaking, but listening intelligently, like a solid young man sure of his strength and taking notes. Later he became more friendly, astounding us by stories of his prowess. Of medium height, stocky, with hard muscles and florid complexion, he was at this time a great oarsman, rowing fifty miles on the Seine in a day for amusement. He was also very proud of his virility and told us incredible tales about women, feats of sexual athleticism which sent Flaubert into great fits of laughter.

"Then we did not even wonder if Maupassant had any talent; of course we heard certain poems of his, written for men only, but it is not very difficult to shine in that field. Consequently, we were surprised when he published a little poem, *Au bord de l'eau*, in which were qualities of the first order, rare simplicity and solidity of technique, revealing a writer already master of his craft. From that moment he began to count with us; he was one of the most gifted of the young men whose growth we were watching, one of those who had the most strength and courage to carry on the work of the century at the point where his elders would leave it."

The end of that apprenticeship had now come. "For seven years I wrote verses, I wrote stories, I wrote novelettes, I even wrote an appalling drama. Of all this nothing remains. The Master read everything, and at lunch the following Sunday he developed his criticisms, gradually driving into my head two or three principles which sum up his long and patient teaching. 'If one has originality,' he used to say, 'it must be brought out; if one has none, it must be acquired.'" Two volumes now stand in evidence of what Maupassant had attempted and what he had done. He had attempted to be a poet, but only Bouilhet, Laure de Maupassant, and Flaubert seem to have been seriously impressed by his poetic gifts. He himself declared that "the poems are the work not of inspiration, but of a man who has thought them out." Those written for masculine consumption, to which Zola refers, may be judged by *Ma Source*, or *La Femme à la Barbe*, which were preserved with other *erotica*, in *La Nouveau Parnasse Satirique du XIXe Siècle*. His contributions to this volume, together with *Les Cousines de la Colonelle*, by the "Vicomtesse de Cœur-Brulant," with a frontispiece by Rops, which appeared in Brussels in 1880, constitute his share in the pornographic literature of the nineteenth century.

This year 1880, which witnessed his successful emergence from obscurity and his release from official drudgery, should have been one of signal pride and happiness. No young author ever had a more triumphant *début* than Maupassant in that spring, when his Master rejoiced with him, and the press, by abuse and appreciation, made him famous overnight. For a few weeks he could forget that dilated pupil in his right eye, and the mysterious manifestations of the hereditary tapeworm in his family. But the fatality which poisoned all his pleasures did not relax on this occasion of his purest joy. Death, which was always to haunt him, threw a deep shadow over these days that seemed so bright.

"Are you going to M. Flaubert on Sunday?" asked Pélagie, Edmond de Goncourt's servant, since famous as "Germinie Lacerteux." As she asked the question, that Saturday morning in May, 1880, Goncourt re-received a telegram: "Flaubert dead." The little world of which he was the centre could hardly believe the news. Maxime du Camp had that day received a letter from Croisset announcing that Flaubert would visit him on the coming Monday. Maupassant also expected him, and was more perturbed by an unfavourable article in *Le Temps* on *Les Soirées de Médan* — " the young

men who call Zola master have his impudence but not
his talent " — than by a thought of impending disaster.
Now the one thing in the world had happened which
could affect him so profoundly that his own affairs
seemed of little moment. "Flaubert certainly carried
with him to the grave the tenderest love I shall ever feel
for any man, the greatest admiration I shall ever have
for any writer, the most absolute veneration that any
human being will ever inspire in me." The "magic
shield" which protected Maupassant was gone. He
telegraphed the news to Zola, and went down to Croisset.

As Flaubert had watched for two nights beside the
corpse of Alfred Le Poittevin and seen him sewn into
his shroud, so Le Poittevin's nephew prepared the dead
body of his Master for the grave in the cemetery at
Rouen, where Louis Bouilhet, the Flauberts, and the
Le Poittevins lay buried.

On the 11th of May, 1880, the funeral took place, and
for the last time he left Croisset with his friends; Banville, Coppée, and Zola acting as pallbearers. Goncourt's refusal to be the fourth placed Maupassant in a
dilemma as to who should have that honour. A journalist from *Le Figaro* claimed it for his paper, but the
faithful Philippe Burty was chosen. The municipality
of Rouen was not represented in the procession of some
twenty people who started out lugubriously along the
towing-path and up the dusty road to the little chapel
where Madame Bovary confessed her sins. The sun
was shining brightly and the walk from there to the
cemetery seemed "interminable" to Edmond de Goncourt, who beguiled his time by observing the mourners:

"In the careless crowd, who find the funeral very
long, the idea of having a little celebration begins to
become manifest. They talk of brill *à la Normande* and

duckling *à l'orange* at Mennechet's, while the names of infamous streets are whispered, accompanied by the blinking leer of amorous tomcats. . . . We arrive at the cemetery, which is full of the perfume of hawthorn, and which overlooks the city, lying buried in a violet shadow that makes it look like a city of slate. As soon as the holy water is sprinkled on the coffin, the thirsty crowd makes a rush for the town, every face beaming with bawdy anticipation. Daudet, Zola, and I leave, refusing to have anything to do with the 'spread' being prepared for the evening, and return talking piously of the dead man."

They wondered why Rouen had not been represented at the funeral. Even at the gates of the city they had still hoped for some token of respect, but there had come only the regulation picket of soldiers to which a dead chevalier of the Legion of Honour is entitled. Zola thought of Marseilles, also a commercial centre, and was sure that its citizens would have turned out in large crowds to do honour to a fellow townsman of Flaubert's stature. As the cortège slowly wound its way through the city, the indifference of the passers-by was the measure of his fame. Up the steep streets to the graveyard they followed the swaying coffin, until it reached the cemetery gates all perfumed with clumps of lilac. There Zola, Daudet, and Goncourt look back at the city beneath. It seemed like a copper cloud fringed with sunshine, and its spires and gables, its flaming Gothic gave it the appearance of a mediæval city. Why, they all wondered, had Flaubert, who had drunk of the Romanticism of 1830, never put that Gothic city, "like the horizon of a ballad by Victor Hugo," into his books?

They recalled the few words spoken by Flaubert's old friend Charles Lapierre at the grave, and how the huge coffin was lowered into the vault by the gravediggers, under the orders of a spectral figure in black "who looked as if he had stepped out *Han d'Islande*." Then the coffin had toppled head forward, and no effort could make it fit. As the wood creaked and the ropes groaned, it hung upside down, and could neither be raised nor lowered. Flaubert's dearly loved niece Caroline sobbed, and friends watched the efforts of the gravediggers, until someone cried: "Enough, enough! Wait until afterwards." And so they had left Flaubert, swinging between heaven and earth.

Émile Bergerat, editor of Charpentier's *Vie Moderne*, Francois Coppée, Théodore de Banville, and others remained to celebrate the occasion in the manner so contemptuously described by Goncourt. To Bergerat and his companions the situation presented itself more politely as "a funeral feast, in the manner of the ancients, at which to discuss again the lofty genius who has gone, and his work, left unfinished, alas!" But when they sat down, there were thirteen at table. Banville, who was "superstition incarnate," turned livid, for he was only two years younger than Flaubert, and saw a sign from heaven that his turn would be next. Coppée pretended a sudden indisposition as an excuse for retiring, and others seemed prepared to follow him. The party threatened to disintegrate, when Bergerat offered to go out into the highways and byways and find a fourteenth guest.

"It would have been simpler," he explains, "to have asked one of my colleagues on the Rouen press, but where could I find one at that hour, when all the offices are empty or closed in the provinces? Besides, to ask people to a funeral repast as stop-gap is to invite a certain snub, even if the person were starving. After a few attempts, which rightly met with harsh rebuffs, I was about to decide to absent myself from the banquet, thus reducing it to the safe number of twelve, when I met by chance a young infantryman on leave, who was gasping at the culinary odours from our restaurant, like Banville's own Gringoire.

"When I briefly explained the service which some celebrated writers from Paris solicited of his good nature, he began to laugh and giggle — 'Gustave Flaubert? Never heard of him. Who's he?' And he turned to walk away. Then he came back and asked me if Francis Coppée was one of our illustrious guests. This was the man he most wanted to see and meet. He knew his *Grève des forgerons* by heart, recited it to his comrades constantly, with great success, and regarded it as the loveliest thing in the world. We were saved! I promised, not only to introduce him to Coppée, but to get him an autographed photograph. I led in our fourteenth man.

"The result was a riot. Théodore de Banville rushed to greet the wandering minstrel, squeezed his hand, called him his dear boy, and swore he would use his influence on his behalf with the Minister of War. We forced him to act as chairman, with the author of *Gringoire* on one side and the author of *La Grève des forgerons* on the other, and the latter saw to it that his admirer's glass was never empty for an instant.

"I am ashamed to confess that, if the soldier boy had never heard of Flaubert, we ourselves — such is the power of contagion — had forgotten the purpose of our pious feast, the journey, the funeral, our dead friend, the great man, and everything else, just as if we were simple citizens of Rouen or members of its Municipal Council. The hero of the hour was an unknown soldier, lured by the smell of duckling *à la rouennaise,* and obviously sent by holy Providence, as Banville assured us, crossing himself."

Like a story in the manner of *La Maison Tellier*, Flaubert's funeral closes a chapter in Maupassant's life. From now on he is thrown back upon himself, and he reverts to his mother as his only confidant, for he is a man with few friends and many acquaintances, feminine in his lack of that comradeship which binds men together in helpful and affectionate intimacy. To Zola he confesses his loss: "I cannot tell you how much I think of Flaubert; he haunts and pursues me. The thought of him recurs to me incessantly. I hear his voice and see his gestures again: every moment he is standing before me in his great brown dressing-gown, with his arms raised, talking to me. A solitude seems to encompass me, the first of those horrible separations which will now continue from year to year, taking away all the people one loves, with whom memories are bound up, with whom one could talk of intimate matters. Such blows bruise the spirit and leave an enduring pain in one's every thought."

All that Maupassant can do now is to prepare *Bouvard et Pécuchet* for publication, the work whose growth he had watched and helped step by step. By the end of the year he has the manuscript ready for Mme. Juliette Adam, and serialization begins in *La Nouvelle Revue*. He can register his peculiar, morbid protest when Maxime du Camp innocently reveals the fact that Flaubert was an epileptic, as though that infliction were a shameful sin; but then, du Camp had the sinister notion that there was "a connection between Flaubert's art and his epilepsy," and he tried to explain the one in terms of the other. In time, however, Maupassant himself asks: "Are people who are quite happy, strong, and healthy, properly equipped to understand, penetrate, and express life, this life of ours so tormented and so short?" And at the height of his own fame he still speculates on the very different career of his Master, "an artist in a state of artistic exaltation," "loving literature in such an absolute manner that there was no room in his soul, filled by this love, for any other ambition." Then he looks into his own soul:

"An artist almost always conceals some secret ambition unrelated to art. Often one pursues glory, the blaze of glory which sets us, during our lifetime, in an apotheosis, turns our heads, excites applause, and captivates the hearts of women. To please the women! That is the ardent desire of practically all of us. By the omnipotence of one's talent, to become in Paris, in the world, an exceptional person, admired, flattered, loved, who can pluck, almost at will, those fruits of living flesh for which we hunger. To be preceded everywhere one goes by renown, respect, and adulation, to see all eyes fixed upon one, and to receive all smiles — that is what we crave, we who take up the strange and difficult profession of interpreting nature by artificial means."

By way of contrast Maupassant likes to remember the simplicity of a great man, fearing and desiring the work which tortured and fascinated him, as he laboured "like a patient and meticulous colossus building a pyramid with a child's marbles." He can see Flaubert "buried in his high-back oak armchair, his head sunk upon his powerful shoulders, his blue eyes resting on the paper, the tiny pupil looking like a black seed perpetually moving. A light silk skull cap, like a bishop's, covers the top of his head, and allows long curls to ripple on his back. A huge dressing-gown of brown cloth completely envelops him, and his red face, marked by a thick white moustache with drooping ends, swells from a wild rush of blood. His glance from the shadow of great dark eyelashes runs over the lines, explores the words, turns phrases inside out, and watches the expression on the faces of the listening authors, noting the effect like a hunter tracking game."

The memory of those meetings in the Rue Murillo never leaves him. When the bell rang and Flaubert had thrown the silk tablecloth over his writing-table to save its contents from prying eyes, the visitors could come in. "Turgenev plunged into an armchair and talked slowly, in a soft voice which was rather feeble and hesitating, but lent an extreme charm and interest to what he said"; "M. Taine, his eyes hidden behind his spectacles, looking very timid, brought historic documents, unknown facts, an odour and taste of ransacked archives"; "then Alphonse Daudet, carrying a whiff of the air of Paris, the gay, bustling, living, rakish Paris. He draws silhouettes that are infinitely funny in a few words, subjecting everyone and everything to his charming irony, so Southern and personal, the delicacy of his vivid wit being emphasized by the charm of his face and his gestures, and the skill of his stories, always as well composed as though he had written them. His handsome, intelligent head is covered by a wave of ebony-black hair reaching to his shoulders, mingling with his curly beard, whose sharp points he often twists. His long but narrow eyes are as black as ink, and have sometimes the vague glance of extremely short sight. His voice sings a little; his gestures are keen, his appearance restless: a real son of the South.

"Émile Zola arrives in his turn, breathless after five flights of stairs, and always followed by his faithful Paul Alexis. He falls into a chair and looks at our faces to see our states of mind, the tone and trend of the conversation. Seated a little apart, with one leg curled under him, nursing his ankle and speaking seldom, he listens attentively. . . . He is of medium height, rather stout, and looks a good-natured obstinate fellow. His head, like those one sees in many old Italian pictures, is not beautiful but shows strength of character and intelligence. His short hair stands up from a very high forehead, and his straight nose, as if clipped by a sudden cut, stops short above a lip shaded by a rather heavy black moustache. The lower part of this plump but energetic face is covered by a closely cropped beard. His black short-sighted, penetrating eyes search, smile, often ironically, while a curious twist raises his upper lip in a funny, mocking way.

"Others arrive: here is Charpentier, the publisher. But for some grey in his long black hair, one would take him for a youth. He is slender and handsome, with a slightly pointed chin, shaded with blue by a heavy beard carefully shaved. He wears only a moustache. He laughs readily with a youthful, sceptical laugh, and promises everything they ask to each writer who pushes him in a corner to make a thousand suggestions. Here is the charming poet, Catulle Mendès, with the face of a sensual and seductive Christ, whose silky blond beard and fair hair surround his pale intelligent features with a fair cloud. An incomparable talker, a refined and subtle artist, catching the most fugitive literary sensations, he pleases Flaubert particularly because of the charm of his conversation and the sharpness of his wit. Here are Émile Bergerat, who married the second daughter of Théophile Gautier, José-Maria de Heredia, the famous sonnetteer, . . . Huysmans, Hennique, Céard. . . .

"Then there enters, usually the last, a man of medium height and slender, whose serious face, though often smiling, has the stamp of pride and nobility. He has long greyish hair which seems to have lost its colour, a moustache somewhat whiter, and curious eyes, the nervous sensitiveness of high breeding. It is Edmond de

Goncourt. He comes forward, holding in one hand a packet of special tobacco which he always keeps with him, offering the other free hand to his friends." And then the arguments were fast and furious, as the apprentice listened to the only literary conversations he could ever stand, for he never frexuented the "Nouvelle Athènes," as George Moore had noticed.

These Sunday gatherings were gone for ever; gone, too, was the eager youth who frequented them, and there learnt the craft which had now transformed him into a rising author of popular successes. Of all who met together, Maupassant alone began at once to rival Daudet and Zola in popularity. The others, whether his elders or contemporaries, never knew the success in terms of money, fame and . . . women (to mention what he prized so highly) which came to the author of *Boule de Suif*. Certainly not the greatest of them all, who "fell at his work-table, killed by his mistress, literature, like all great lovers who are consumed by their passion," as Maupassant put it in characteristic image. Yet, to the end it was Flaubert's example that lived before him; not that of Zola, from whom he diverged as soon as conveniently possible, or of Goncourt, who saw through him, or of Daudet, in whose circle his name rarely occurs. In one of the last lucid intervals before his own brief life closed, Maupassant's thoughts were back with his old Master. "I always think of poor Flaubert, and I say to myself that I should like to die, if I were sure that someone would think of me in this way." But what was there in the man or his work to justify that hope?

CHAPTER IV

INITIATION

IMMEDIATELY after Flaubert's death Maupassant turned to Zola for help. "I am asking you to do me a service, which you were the first to promise," he wrote, before leaving the ministry of Public Instruction; "that is, to say a few words about my book of poems in your article in the *Voltaire*. I have had a review from the *Globe*, from the *National*, from Banville, favourable mention twice in *Le Temps*, an excellent article in the Marseilles *Sémaphore*, one in the *Revue Politique et littéraire*, and good notices in *Le Petit Journal*, *Le XIXe Siècle*, etc., etc.; last night a lecture from Sarcey.

"It is selling well, and the first edition is almost exhausted, but I shall need a good drive to get rid of the 200 copies that remain. The second edition is ready. Laffitte has asked me for a story which I am writing. I did not name a price, as I wanted to consult you about it. Further, the *Gaulois* has taken me on its staff, also Huysmans. Each of us to write one article a week, and we get 500 francs a month."

Without Flaubert, "The Five" as they were called — Flaubert, Daudet, Goncourt, Turgenev, and Zola — began gradually to surrender their maïeutic functions. Another group, the smaller Five — Guy de Maupassant, J. K. Huysmans, Henry Céard, Léon Hennique, and Paul Alexis, already known to the newspapers as "Zola's train" — had now attained a sort of corporate existence through the publication of *Les Soirées de Médan*. As a matter of course, Zola's relation to the group became analogous to that of Flaubert, but it was never identical, because the circumstances of the association were not those of a master and his disciples, but rather those of equals. There was the same easy intimacy between the younger men and their elder as between themselves, for the differences of age were not so marked as in the case of the Big Five. All, save Maupassant, had become acquainted with Zola independently of Flaubert, and it was through Paul Alexis, "Zola's shadow," that he came into contact with this group of his contemporaries. For a time Zola's Thursday evenings supplemented Flaubert's Sunday nights, and excursions to Médan took the place of those to Croisset.

Ever since the ignominious end of the Franco-Prussian war, sentimental songs and stories, with *Revanche* for their theme, consoled the patriotism of the populace. Ten years later Remy de Gourmont was to make a final disavowal of this chauvinism in the famous article *Le joujou patriotisme*, which caused his dismissal from the Bibliothèque Nationale. At this time the heresy known to-day as defeatism was whispered only in select circles, and such manifestos as Abel Hermant's *Le Cavalier Miserey* or Lucien Descaves's *La Caserne* and *Sous-Offs* were still some years away. It was, however, the duty of all true Naturalists to shatter the cherished illusions of the bourgeoisie, and what could be more tempting than the tearful patriotism of the *Revenchards?* So, as the five disported themselves on the banks of the Seine at Médan, the idea of a volume sardonically illustrating various aspects of the Franco-Prussian war took shape.

The material for such a work was almost all ready to hand. Zola had published *L'Attaque du moulin*, and Céard *La Saignée*, in Petersburg periodicals; Huysmans had written *Sac-au-Dos* for a Brussels weekly; Hen-

nique's *L'Affaire de Grand Sept* was complete in manuscript; Alexis was writing *Après la bataille*. All that
remained was for Maupassant to find a subject, and
Boule de Suif was the result. A title for the book presented some difficulties. Huysmans suggested *L'Invasion comique*, but this seemed too unpatriotic, so the
non-committal and unpromising title of *Les Soirées de
Médan* was chosen, as a compliment to Zola. And in
order to arouse the critics, Maupassant sent to the
Gaulois an advance article facetiously describing the
genesis of the forthcoming work, but serving also as
manifesto:

"We make no claim to being a school. We are just a
group of friends who were drawn to Zola by our common
admiration for him, and who have since drawn closer
and closer together by an affinity of temperaments, a
great similarity of ideas on all subjects, and the same
philosophical tendencies. For my own part, having no
position as a writer, how can I claim to belong to a
school? I admire without distinction whatever seems
to me superior in all centuries and in all *genres*. There
is, however, an obvious and fatal reaction which has
unconsciously taken place in us against the Romantic
spirit, for the sole reason that literary generations follow but never resemble each other.

"Romanticism has produced immortal works of art,
but what shocks us is merely the results of its philosophy. We complain because the work of Hugo has
partly destroyed the work of Voltaire and Diderot. The
old wisdom of Montaigne and Rabelais has almost died
out of the land, thanks to the bombastic sentimentalism
of the Romantics, their dogmatic denial of right and
logic. They have substituted the idea of forgiveness
for the idea of justice, spreading amongst us a sentimental and pitying softness which has taken the place

of reason. Thanks to them, the theatres are filled by gentlemen of shady character and strumpets who are shocked by the presence on the stage of a common scoundrel. It is the morality of Romanticism in the mob which often compels the courts to acquit touching criminals, male and female, who have no excuse.

"For the great masters of this school (since it is a school) I have a boundless admiration, against which my reason often revolts, for I believe that Schopenhauer and Herbert Spencer have many sounder ideas about life than the illustrious author of *Les Misérables*. — That is the only criticism I should dare to make, and here it is not a question of literature. — From a literary standpoint what appears detestable to us are the old tearful barrel-organs, whose mechanism was invented by Jean Jacques Rousseau, and whose handles have been ceaselessly turned by a whole line of novelists — of whom M. Feuillet, I hope, is the last — grinding out invariably the same false and sentimental tunes.

"As for the quarrels about the words 'realism' and 'idealism,' I do not understand them. An inflexible law of philosophy teaches us that we can imagine nothing save what touches our senses, and a proof of this powerlessness is the stupidity of what are called ideal conceptions, of the paradises invented by all religions. We have but one objective, therefore: Man and Life, which must be interpreted artistically. If one cannot express these in a manner both correct and artistically superior, it is for lack of talent.

"When a gentleman who is called realist strives to write as well as possible, and is incessantly preoccupied with questions of art, he is, in my sense, an idealist. As for those who profess to make life more beautiful than nature — as if one could conceive it other than it is — to bring down heaven to earth, and who write 'for women only,' they are either charlatans or fools, at least in my opinion. I adore fairy-tales, I may add, but in their own domain they have to be more convincing than any novel of contemporary manners.

"Now for some notes on our volume:

"We used to meet in summer at Zola's house in Médan. During the lengthy process of digesting long meals (for we are all *gourmands* and *gourmets*, and Zola alone eats as much as three ordinary novelists), we used to talk. He told us about the novels he was going to write, his literary ideas, his opinions on all sorts of subjects. Sometimes he would take his rifle, which he handled as shortsighted men do, and while talking, he would fire at clumps of grass which we told him were birds, and his astonishment was considerable when he found no booty. On certain days we went fishing. Then Hennique distinguished himself, greatly to the despair of Zola, who caught nothing but old boots.

"I used to lie stretched out in his boat *Nana,* or I went swimming for hours, while Paul Alexis wandered around with his bawdy ideas, Huysmans smoked cigarettes, and Céard, who thought the country stupid, was bored to tears.

"Thus the afternoons passed, but, as the nights were magnificent, warm, full of the perfume of leaves, we used to go every evening and stroll about the large island opposite. I rowed them all across in *Nana.*

"One moonlight night we were talking about Merimée, whom the ladies call 'a charming story-teller!' when Huysmans spoke a few words more or less to the following effect: 'A story-teller is a gent who, not knowing how to write, talks pretentious piffle.' Then we came to going over all the celebrated story-tellers, and to praising those who told their stories *viva voce,* the most marvellous, to our knowledge, being the great Russian, Turgenev, who is almost a French writer. Paul Alexis declared that a story is a very difficult thing to get down on paper. Céard, the sceptic, gazed at the moon and murmured: 'There is a lovely piece of romantic scenery. Someone should use it . . .' 'For a sentimental story,' added Huysmans. But Zola thought it was an excellent idea and that we should tell each other stories. The suggestion made us laugh, and we agreed, in order to make it more difficult, that the framework first chosen should be preserved by all who followed, and used for different adventures.

"We all sat down, and amidst the immense calm of the drowsy fields, beneath the brilliant light of the moon, Zola related that terrible chapter from the sinister history of war called *L'Attaque du moulin*. When he had finished, each of us cried: 'You must write that at once! He laughed and said: 'It is written!'

"The next day it was my turn. The day after, Huysmans amused us greatly with his story of the troubles of a reluctant militiaman. Retelling the siege of Paris, with fresh details, Céard unfolded a tale full of philosophy, if not true, then, at least, convincing, and always real ever since the ancient poem of Homer. If women eternally inspire men to foolish actions, the warriors whom they especially favour with their attentions necessarily pay a greater penalty than other men.

"Hennique demonstrated once again that men, who are often intelligent and reasonable when taken separately, infallibly become brutes when they are in a crowd. This is what might be called collective madness. I know of nothing funnier and more horrible, at the same time, than the siege of that brothel and the massacre of the unfortunate prostitutes. — Paul Alexis could not find a subject and kept us waiting four days. He wanted to tell us stories about Prussians who violated corpses, but our exasperation silenced him. Finally he conceived the amusing tale of a society lady going to find her husband, who has fallen on the field of honour, and allowing herself to be 'moved' by a poor wounded soldier — this soldier being a priest.

"Zola thought these stories were curious and proposed that we should make a book of them."

Henry Céard, who wrote the more sober preface to *Les Soirées de Médan*, described Maupassant's manifesto as "more astute than truthful," and "designed to astonish the boobies and set them talking" about "five unknown writers, in the wake of an author of established reputation, who decide to appear together between the covers of one volume in the booksellers' windows." In his own preface Céard melodramatically announced: "We are prepared for all sorts of attacks, for the deliberate misrepresentation and the ignorance of which the critics of the moment have already given us so many proofs." And in this he was not far wrong, for Maupassant certainly stirred up the journalistic animals.

Albert Wolff, in the *Figaro*, at once rose to the bait set in the *Gaulois*, and declared that these people wrote as absurdly as they had talked at Médan, "and it is this band of young whippersnappers who, in a preface of rare insolence, throw down the gauntlet to the critics . . . *Les Soirées de Médan* does not deserve a single line of criticism. Save for Zola's story, with which the volume opens, it is the last word in mediocrity." Already Flaubert had been consoled by Jean Richepin's statement, in *Gil Blas*, that these writers used Flaubert's name "very much as if a pig were to invoke the name of Saint Anthony," and he had told his niece to be sure to read Richepin's "verdict on Zola's henchmen, which is perfect."

In *L'Evènement* the "feverish vanity " of the Naturalists was the text of an indignant discourse. "They have just published a volume, *Les Soirées de Médan*, with a preface of some twenty lines. This preface is simply an insult, but that is not particularly surprising. . . . In addition to being very badly constructed, this preface is so unconsciously idiotic that it will charm connoisseurs of our old French humour." Édouard Rod, on the other hand, was sympathetic: "The union of these young men is strength. Undoubtedly it will disturb the violent opponents of Naturalism, those who try to be funny instead of trying to understand, who laugh at them instead of reading them. On the contrary, those who are interested in the modern movement will greet with pleasure this collective work of theirs, which shows both promise and actual achievement."

Zola himself regarded *Boule de Suif* as the one important feature of the volume, yet Maupassant was never at any time a member of the Naturalistic school. So long as Flaubert was alive, he and Maupassant were privately much amused by Zola's pronunciamentos on the subject of Naturalism, the "experimental novel," and so forth, although they dissembled their amusement to Zola himself, and tactfully praised him to his face. Consequently, the innocent author of *L'Assommoir* and *Nana*, which had just brought him fame and prosperity after his years of hunger and struggle, saw no reason why he should not count young M. de Maupassant as his most promising and distinguished pupil. He had immediately complied with the request for an article on *Des Vers*, although greatly upset by Flaubert's death and the funeral at Rouen. "Your letter," he wrote, "reached me just as I was beginning the article, which must have appeared this morning. I am still so much shaken by the journey to Rouen that I am not thinking very well. However, I wanted to keep my promise, and if the article is not very good, do not blame me. I did it chiefly with a view to helping sales. — I, too, cannot get rid of the thought of Flaubert. At night, before going asleep, I always see him. But, as you say, we must accustom ourselves to death, for every day now it will take from us something of ourselves and of others."

When Manet took George Moore to the ball at the Élysée Montmartre, which was given in honour of the company playing *L'Assommoir* at the Ambigu Theatre, his purpose was to see the author of *Flowers of Passion*, dressed in the cap and blouse of a Parisian workman, exercising his barbaric French on Hélène Petit, who played Gervaise so successfully, the rôle for which Maupassant's friend Suzanne Lagier had "slenderized" in vain. The golden-haired young Irishman, as yet untried in the art of prose fiction, was a fervent admirer, and had come to meet Zola and participate in his success. Maupassant, on the other hand, had thought the play "interminable and not very effective," but it was a great advertisement for Naturalism, and laid the foundations of the popularity of which Zola's disciples were glad to avail themselves a year later. George Moore, at least, was frankly an adherent of the Naturalistic movement, and, having failed to get any conversation with Zola at the ball, he journeyed down to Médan.

Up many staircases of polished oak, past "Japanese prints depicting furious fornication," he was led, "after many tedious explanations" to Madame Zola, into the presence of the great man, who, "untucking his fat leg," informed his shy visitor that Protestantism had never

produced great art. At the same time he expressed
his unbounded (but obviously illogical) respect for the
art of George Eliot. By the time *A Mummer's Wife*
appeared as evidence of the pupil's aptitude for Naturalism, Moore had recovered so far from his earlier
reverence that his facetiousness deprived him of the
preface which Zola had promised to write for the French
edition. To no purpose the unhappy author of *Confes-
sions of a Young Man* argued that his gibes at Goncourt
were meant seriously — "he isn't a friend " — but not
the frivolous remarks about Naturalism. "You admit
in your book that you owe your first inspiration to me.
I am proud that this is so, and thank you for saying it.
I am sorry you have changed your opinions; after all
it is the eternal law — children devour their fathers.
I make no complaint. Nature has willed it so." Whereupon George Moore departed, feeling a distinct sensation of inferiority — "the man is greater than his
books " — and he and Alexis mourned the loss of the
preface which was to recoup the latter for revising the
translation. However, "it is Charpentier's funeral,"
as Alexis sagely concluded. "A thousand francs for
corrections."

Maupassant was more fortunate in that his heresies
were not revealed until the moment had long since
passed when Zola could help or hinder his popularity.
The years preceding the publication of *Boule de Suif*
had been *L'Assommoir* and *Nana* years, during which
storms of controversy raged in all the periodicals,
pamphlets innumerable on Zola were published, Gali-
paux recited *En r'venant de l'Assommoir*, to the huge delight of his audiences, while parodies were performed at
the theatres, and Léon Hennique lectured in the Salle
des Conférences on the Boulevard des Capucines —
filling Flaubert and Maupassant with contemptuous

disgust. Victor Hugo was pontificating; Mallarmé
had presented *L'Après-midi d'un Faune;* a young assistant of Leconte de Lisle at the Senate Library had
issued *Les Noces Corinthiennes;* Richepin's blasphemies
in *La Chanson des Gueux* had been reproved; the Dick-
ensian sweetness of Daudet's *Jack* had been transferred
to the theatre. Hector Malot's *Sans Famille* could be
put "into all hands," and *La Fille Élisa* had again irritated a public to whom the mere name of Goncourt
seemed to be a permanent incitement to stupidity.
These years had not been exactly unproductive in
French literature, yet every work was overshadowed by
the portentous rise of Émile Zola, and many were lost
in the endless disputes to which his books and his theories gave rise. "Useful enemies," said Paul Alexis,
giving thanks, "have they not revealed our existence to
the crowd, drawn attention to our works, and prepared
the way for our success? "

When the project was first conceived, Maupassant
was most unwilling to be associated with any formal
pronouncement in favour of Naturalism. "I have been
thinking of our manifesto," he wrote, "and I feel I must
make a complete confession of my literary faith. I believe no more in Naturalism than in Realism or Romanticism. In my view these words are absolutely devoid
of meaning and merely lead to quarrels between opposite
temperaments. . . . Why limit oneself? The Naturalistic is as limited as the fantastic." Maupassant
evidently foresaw what actually happened, for he continued: "Of course, this letter must not go outside our
circle, and I should be in despair if you showed it to
Zola, of whom I am very fond and whom I admire
heartily, for he might perhaps take offence at it. We
must seriously consider the ways to success. Five of
us together can do a great deal, and perhaps there are

some 'stunts' that have never yet been employed. Could we not lay siege to some paper for six months, showering it with articles, requests from friends, and so forth, until we have got one of us properly established there? We shall have to find something unexpected, which will make a stir, and compel public attention. Why not something amusing? A really witty attack. Well, we shall see."

Maupassant is evidently torn between his desire to profit by the immense interest in the doings of Zola and his school and his respect for Flaubert's judgment, which had always been unfavourable to the theory of Naturalism. While he was still writing only verse, his father had shown him a letter from a woman who said: "I wish that a lovely lady with silk stockings and pretty heels and amber-blond hair would teach him all that Flaubert and Zola do not know in matters of that perfection of taste which makes poets and poetry immortal." And the son wrote indignantly to his mother: "I find this sentence a marvel because it sums up all the eternal stupidity of the fair ladies of France. Literature with pretty heels! I know that sort of thing and do not intend to write it. My one desire is to be lacking in that kind of taste, as all great men have been, but to invent a new kind. In my opinion the seventeenth century is the least interesting. It had no Rabelais, no Montaigne, no d'Aubigné, no Régnier, and no Voltaire . . . and all these are greater, I think, than Molière and Corneille. As for the nineteenth century, if our idiotic contemporaries cannot appreciate it, posterity will."

As a matter of historical fact, Maupassant's appearance under the ægis of Zola was adventitious, for, if it was at Médan that the title of *Les Soirées* was decided, the stories themselves had their genesis at Maupassant's apartment. Alexis, Huysmans, Hennique, Céard, and he met in that famous house in the rue Clauzel where, Félicien Champsaur noticed, women appeared at the doors on every floor when gentlemen visitors walked upstairs. Each read his story in turn, Maupassant being the last, and then they drew lots as to the order in which the stories should be printed following Zola's contribution, which had first place. They all agreed that *Boule de Suif* was the best story in the volume, and congratulated Maupassant on his remarkable achievement — an unusual case where friends accurately anticipated the judgment of posterity. Edmond de Goncourt even went so far as to alter for the second time his original list of the future members of the Goncourt Academy. His first choice, in 1874, had been Flaubert, Paul de Saint-Victor, Louis Veuillot, Théodore de Banville, Barbey d'Aurevilly, Eugène Fromentin, Philippe de Chennevières, Émile Zola, Alphonse Daudet, and Léon Cladel. The death of Fromentin had led to the substitution of Paul Bourget's name, and now, instead of Flaubert, came Maupassant. The vogue of "Zola's train" was such that soon Huysmans replaced Chennevières and Henry Céard succeeded Saint-Victor in 1881. Such, however, is the fragility of literary friendships that by 1887 Céard was eliminated, and he did not become a member of the Goncourt Academy until he was elected in 1918. Death and the French Academy had accounted for Barbey d'Aurevilly, Daudet, Banville, Bourget, and Loti, so that in 1900, when the Goncourt Academy finally came into existence, only Huysmans and Hennique represented the heroic age of Naturalism. The unfortunate Zola, because of his "perpetual candidature " for the French Academy, was ruled out in favour of Octave Mirbeau, who, but for his absorption in politics, would have been a sixth contributor to *Les Soirées de Médan*.

Edmond de Goncourt's estimate of Maupassant was never very high — "a remarkable *novelliere*, a most charming story-teller, but a stylist, a great writer — no, never!" — but his choice of him as Flaubert's successor is evidence of the immediate fame achieved by the author of *Boule de Suif*. Maupassant was at once nominated to that succession by critical opinion, partly because of his literary relationship to Flaubert and partly because he was being used as a foil to Zola. Brunetière hastened to absolve him from the charges of brutality, obscenity, and æsthetic blindness which lay against the Naturalistic novelists; alone of the group Maupassant was found worthy. Zola's comment was simple and characteristic. "When our volume reached me I read the story and was delighted with it. It is certainly the best of the six. It has an audacity, a dignity, a subtlety, and a clarity of analysis which make it a little masterpiece. . . . He owes much to Flaubert, it is true . . . but he has an originality of his own which was visible in his first verses and is now confirmed by his prose. . . . His is assuredly one of the best balanced and healthiest temperaments among the younger generation. Now he must write a novel, a sustained work, which will give the measure of his talents."

Zola's own contribution to the volume, long since established as a school text for foreign students of French, was the least Naturalistic, and it became a lyric drama later on without suffering many changes. Céard subsequently disowned *La Saignée*, saying that only the description of the siege of Paris had any merit, but the general and his mistress are in the authentic tradition of *Nana* or *La Curée*. Huysmans came close to the spirit of modern war stories with his conception of a soldier who finds an attack of dysentery a happy relief from the aimless stupidities and cruelties of war. Although Hennique was advised by Zola to "avoid un-usual subjects and adventures that are too startling," he wrote his sardonic account of the heroic capture of a brothel and the destruction of its inhabitants. Paul Alexis could do no better than to adapt the fable of the Matron of Ephesus to the requirements of Naturalism. A story less original than *Boule de Suif* might well have have shone in the dingy setting of *Les Soirées de Médan*.

Maupassant's advantage was reflected in the imme-diate demand for his writings, to which he referred in his letter to Zola, when he said that the *Gaulois* had offered to pay him five hundred francs a month for a weekly article. On the 31st of May, 1880, he began the series of sketches, known as *Les Dimanches d'un bour-geois de Paris*, which appeared every Monday for ten weeks. With Flaubert's pair of typical bourgeois evi-dently in mind, he made the series hinge upon the say-ings and doings of a certain M. Patissot, an obscure and idiotic Civil Servant, who makes an excursion every Sunday to some unfamiliar part of Paris and its envi-rons. There is much laboured humour in the conception of this figure, his elaborate walking outfit, more appro-priate to mountaineering than to his purpose, his plati-tudinous ideas, and his fatuous comments, and a great lack of inventiveness in the setting of his futile adven-tures. In one instance a description of Meissonier's house at Poissy and Zola's at Médan help to eke out Maupassant's slender material. Only the writer's popu-lar vogue at the moment could explain the publication of these laborious attempts to embroider upon the themes of Bouvard and Pécuchet. Maupassant himself wisely consigned them to the limbo of his journalistic writings, and utilized only one situation, the visit of Patissot to his henpecked friend Boivin, in a later story, *Monsieur Mongilet*.

Posthumously these sketches were published in the collected edition of his works, although the same dubious service was not performed for *Dr. Héraclius Gloss*, which has not yet been admitted to the canon of his writings. It is difficult to understand why this much more mature and interesting story, actually his earliest and longest piece of sustained narrative, should have been excluded from the posthumous writings collected by his representatives. It reveals the author's inexperience only in the haste and incoherence to which certain anachronisms must be attributed. The scene is laid in the seventeenth century, yet there are references to the postal service, to gendarmes, and to the prefecture — all later institutions. What is of the greatest interest, however, is the promise in this work of development in a very different direction from that which the success of *Boule de Suif* induced the author to take.

The theme reminds one of Voltaire, and the central figure is sketched in with strokes which have something of the skill of an Anatole France in his portraits of learned eccentrics. Héraclius Gloss is one of the tribe, a *gourmet* and a bibliophile. Intellectually he is a philosopher, a trifle mad, no doubt, and his life is shared among his love of the fair sex, the pursuit of rare tomes, and the quest for truth. As befits the age in which he lives, the good Doctor finds truth in the shape of a dusty manuscript, inscribed in six languages, and bearing a message which converts him to a belief in metempsychosis. Like Peer Gynt, Héraclius Gloss finds first a disciple, and then an opponent, amongst his fellow inmates in a lunatic asylum, but, unlike that of Ibsen's hero, his escape to sanity is of brief duration. When he is locked up again, he re-enters a mad world, which is divided into partisans of his own illusions and those of his adversary. His dog wails outside the gates of the asylum, trying vainly to enter "this house to which only man has the right of entry."

Begun in 1875, this story was laid aside at a time when demands for his work were many, and although he constantly reworked previous manuscripts, *Dr. Héraclius Gloss* was never used, yet never discarded. It would assuredly have suited one of the monthly reviews — Mme. Adam's *Nouvelle Revue*, for example — better than the rehashed sketches from *Gil Blas* and the *Gaulois*, which he often used for his longer contributions to the magazines in the absence of new material. Possibly he was deterred at this stage in his career by the thought which so obviously preoccupied his relatives forty years later, when they hesitatingly allowed *Dr. Héraclius Gloss* to appear in the *Revue de Paris*. Here again is evidence - - the earliest manifestation — of that morbid dread of insanity which was to show, ever more and more insistently, through *Le Horla, Lui? Qui sait?*, until it culminated in the achievement of his destiny at Passy, in the house from which the Princesse de Lamballe saw Louis XVI taken on his last journey to Paris.

It was easier for Maupassant, in this year 1880, to abandon M. Patissot and, without resuscitating Dr. Héraclius Gloss, to satisfy the demands of his editors by writing a series of articles on Corsica. Like most of his journalistic writings, these four articles were not collected by him for publication in book form, but, unlike *Les Dimanches d'un bourgeois de Paris*, they had at least the merit of being competent journalism, and their posthumous inclusion in the same volume with *Au Soleil* does not seem incongruous. He recorded his first impressions of Corsica, which was to be the setting of part of *Une Vie*, and of *Le Bonheur* in *Contes du jour et de la nuit*, and he obtained material for *Une Vendetta* in the same collection of stories, for *Un bandit corse* in *Le Père Milon*, and the vendetta incident in *Une Vie*. If little has been preserved of this period of intense productivity, the germ of later works lay in almost every one of these early contributions to the *Gaulois* and *Gil Blas*.

He wrote his memories of Flaubert in half-a-dozen articles before remoulding the material for the fine preface to the Quantin edition of *Bouvard et Pécuchet* in 1885. Schopenhauer provided him with a theme that suited his mood of pessimism, and Turgenev was presented to Maupassant's readers as "the inventor of the word nihilism." His intentions in regard to these foreign authors had been more ambitious; he wanted to do a series, beginning with Turgenev, but the latter's unexpected modesty proved an obstacle. "After thinking the matter over, I do not want you to write this article about me. You would do it admirably, with tact and restraint, yet I am afraid — if I may say so — that it might be regarded as a piece of friendly advertisement. Seriously, I have not enough readers in France to justify a special article. In any case, if you want to write a series in the *Gaulois* on great foreign authors — an idea of which I approve very much and for which you may call upon me freely if you require information, etc. — I must ask you to include me in my proper rank and turn. In Russia, for example, begin with Pushkin and Gogol; with Dickens in England; in Germany with Goethe, whom Barbey d'Aurevilly has just been so stupidly belittling. If these are liked, then you can pass on to the *dii minorum gentium*." Maupassant had to wait three years, until Turgenev's death, before writing the essay in question, and the series did not materialize.

Instead, like a true Frenchman, Maupassant confined himself to his own friends and compatriots: Goncourt, Bouilhet, Flaubert, Zola, Madame Pasca, and the circle

of Juliette Adam. In the last letter which he wrote to
his publisher Ollendorff, he talked of making a volume of
his literary essays, but only the study of Flaubert was
finally reprinted in his collected works. Literary criticism was not his *métier*, and although he saluted Rod
and Hervieu when they were quite unknown, his articles
on literature were usually dictated by considerations of
personal interest. Some of the books which he formally
sponsored by means of prefaces were curious and characteristic: René Maizeroy's *Celles qui osent* and *La Grande
Bleue; L'Amour à trois,* by Paul Ginisty; *Fille de Fille,* by
Jules Guérin. Addressing M. Guérin with the familiar
tu, he complained that "we are no longer allowed to
speak frankly of the conjunction of the sexes, an act as
useful to the race and as innocent in itself as eating; we
cannot speak of procreation, childbirth, of what are
called the genital functions, although they are as natural
and more simple than what are called intellectual functions, without arousing a hurricane of indignation in the
prudish public." Like so many of the publications of
Henry Kistemaechers, *Fille de Fille* took advantage of
the immunity conferred by Brussels from the excessive
virtue of official France, and Maupassant rejoiced particularly in the image of a faded prostitute whose corset
contained her "as a carafe contains water."

For Cherbuliez, an idol of the moment, he had the
contempt of the average French critic when confronted
with the French of a Swiss, or even a Belgian, writer,
and he denied to Juliette Adam, as to all women authors,
a real sense of style. In the absence of a series of articles
on foreigners, Maupassant contrived in five articles to
deal with a number of his contemporaries, apart from
the "Five," who were the friends of his Master. Catulle
Mendès and Paul Bourget are alarmingly coupled under
the title of *Les Subtils,* while Hennique and Maizeroy

are *Les Audacieux*. Having objected to Stendhal and Balzac on the ground that they were not stylists, Maupassant could appreciate the subtle charm of *Celles qui osent* and *La Fange*. Huysmans also pleased him, but Loti was too romantic, and an article in *Gil Blas* demonstrated the absurdity of crediting Breton peasants with the lofty sentiments of *Pécheur d'Islande*. Anatole France is noted as a "charming and delicate" frequenter of Madame Adam's salon, where he was still a modest Parnassian, author of a virtuous novel crowned by the French Academy, and as yet unacquainted with the discipline of Madame Arman de Caillavet, who made an author and a gentleman of him.

In a more typical vein than these literary judgments were Maupassant's other contributions to the press. About the time of his return from Corsica in the autumn of 1880, *Le Gaulois* published *Conseils d'une grand'mère*, in which the author's own apologia for physical pleasure is thrown into the form of a contrast between the romantic monogamy of a modern young girl and the philosophical polyandry of a lady of the old *régime*. It was fittingly included in the definitive edition of *La Maison Tellier*, the book on which he was then working. He himself did not reprint it, and when the volume appeared the following year, only two stories had previously been published, *Histoire d'une fille de ferme* and *En Famille*. Juliette Adam had at last admitted Flaubert's disciple to *La Nouvelle Revue* by publishing the latter story in February, 1881, much to Turgenev's satisfaction, as he mentions in a letter regretting to hear of Maupassant's bad health.

In order to work at his second volume of stories he retired to his mother's house at Étretat, where even the imminence of that event could not chase away his melancholy: "I am writing to you at the corner of the table

in our little drawing-room. The two dogs, grown thin,
but lively and well, are lying at my feet; Matho keeps
interrupting me by rubbing against my leg. Daphne is
quite cured. But I sneeze and blow my nose, in the grip
of an awful cold, for I travelled all night in a tempera-
ture of five degrees, and I cannot get warm in our frozen
house. The cold wind blows in under the doors, the
lamp is burning low, and the light comes from the fire, a
fire which toasts my face but does not warm the room.
All the old things are about me, sad and dreary. Not
a sound is heard from the village in the lifelessness of
winter. Even the sea is silent.

"The loneliness of life chills me more than the solitude
of the house. I feel a vast scattering of all living beings,
the burden of emptiness. And in the midst of this retreat of everything my brain works lucidly, precisely,
dazzling me with the eternal Nothing. This sounds like
a phrase of Father Hugo's, but it would take a long
time to express my clear idea in clear language — another proof that the bombast of the Romantics is due to
lack of hard work. But it is cold and very miserable. . . ."

And after the inevitable hiatus of family censorship,
we are allowed to read: "I have almost finished my
story about the women from the brothel at first communion. I think it is at least as good as *Boule de Suif*, if
not better."

He wrote in January, 1881, and in the spring *La Maison Tellier* was published, but Maupassant could not
wait to enjoy the reception of it. His eyes were troub-
ling him again, and chronic iritis was diagnosed by some
doctors. He took flight to Algeria, craving sunlight
and joy, but in a mood of the deepest pessimism. "Life,
which is so short and so long, becomes intolerable at
times. It unfolds, always the same, and ends in death.

We cannot stop it, nor change it, nor understand it, and often the futility of one's effort fills one with angry rebellion. Whatever we may do, we must die! Whatever we believe, whatever we think, whatever we try to do, we must die. It seems as if we are about to die to-morrow without knowing anything more, yet disgusted by what we do know. Then we feel crushed by a feeling of 'the eternal wretchedness of all things,' of human impotence, of the monotony of every action.

"We get up, we walk, we lean at the window. The people opposite are lunching, as they lunched yesterday, as they will lunch to-morrow: the father, the mother, four children. Three years ago the grandmother was still with them. She has gone. The father has greatly changed since we have been neighbours. He does not notice it. He seems satisfied. He seems happy. The fool!

"They talk about a marriage, about a death; then about the chicken, which is tender, and the servant, who is dishonest. They worry about a thousand useless and foolish things. Idiots!

"The sight of their flat, where they have been living for eighteen years, disgusts and irritates me. Is that life? Four walls, two doors, a window, a bed, some chairs, a table — that's all! A prison! A prison! Any place where one lives a long time becomes a prison. Oh, to escape, to go away! To flee from the familiar places, the people, the movements, which are the same at the same hours, and specially the same thoughts.

"When one is tired; tired of weeping from morning till night; tired of not having the strength to get up and drink a glass of water; tired of friends' faces that one sees too often and that have become irritating, of odious and placid neighbours, of familiar and monotonous things, the house, the street, the servant who comes in and asks 'What do you want for dinner?' and who goes out, kicking the ragged hem of her dirty skirt with her run-down heels, at every step; tired of the too faithful dog, of the changeless spots on the hangings, of the regularity of the meals, of sleeping in the same bed, of every action repeated every day; tired of oneself, of one's own voice, of the things one always repeats, of the narrow circle of one's ideas; tired of seeing one's face in the mirror, of the grimaces while shaving, while combing one's hair — then one must go away and enter a new and changing life.

"Travelling is a kind of door through which one emerges from known reality into an unexplored reality which seems like a dream. A railway station! A harbour! The whistle of a train and the first puff of its steam! A great liner passing slowly by the piers, its belly throbbing with impatience, on its flight to new countries off on the horizon! Who can see these without a thrill of longing, without feeling in one's soul the exciting desire for long journeys?"

Maupassant left Paris on the 6th of July 1881, "drawn by an imperious desire for Africa, by the nostalgia of the unknown Desert, as if by the presentiment of a passion about to be born." He describes the crossing from Marseilles to Algiers, the devastating effect of French customs; then the Province of Oran. After that comes Bou-Amama, "that elusive scoundrel who, having terrorized our African army, disappeared so completely that people are beginning to believe he never existed." He reached the Province of Algiers, and was inspired by the Ramadan, and by the "courtesans of the desert," and stirred to ingenuous speculations as to the reasons for the existence of Socratic morals amongst the Arabs. He joined a military expedition into the desert, discovered that the Arabs kill their relations if the

latter become insane, and learned how to suffocate a
toad by making it smoke a cigarette. He cast a discon-
solate glance at the corruption of the French adminis-
tration and at the Arab women, "small, white as milk,
with the expression of young sheep," and noticed that
by looking at them in profile he could see more of them
than they intended should meet the eye. His journey
ended at Constantine, where he admired the beautiful
Jewesses, and was amused by the precocious little girls
in their picturesque costumes. "One would think it
was a country in a fairy-tale, a country of tiny ladies of
easy virtue . . . a boarding school of ten-year-old
courtesans, seeds of love just budding."

The adventure was strenuous, but after a few weeks
he had driven away the shadows that had haunted him.
He began to think of Paris and his book. "Just a line."
he wrote to his mother in August, "to tell you that I am
in excellent health. . . . In an hour I leave for Algiers,
where at last I shall find letters and newspapers, for I
have received nothing since I left there. I am standing
the heat very well, and I can tell you it was pretty bad
on the high plains. One whole day we travelled through
the sirocco, which blew fire into our faces. We could not
touch the barrels of our rifles, which burned our hands.
There were scorpions under every stone, and we saw
jackals and dead camels which were being torn to pieces
by vultures. An officer of the zouaves, whom we met
with a detachment in the middle of the desert, told me
that Zola had written an article about me in *Le Figaro*."

At Algiers he found a letter from Turgenev, who had
just got back from Russia: "Your name is making a
stir in Russia. They have translated everything that
was translatable, and I have brought back a tremendous
article on you (in the *Golos*), very well written and most
enthusiastic." It was time to go back to that life from

which he had fled just as it was smiling at him.   He could write about his journey in the *Gaulois*, reserving the business of making a book of *Au Soleil* until a couple of years later.   Perhaps, despite the pain in his eyes, and the nightmares which he had recorded in his new book, and the congenial philosophy of Schopenhauer, he could enjoy the fame for which he had waited so patiently, and for which *La Maison Tellier* was his deliberate bid, the first book of prose for which he alone was responsible.   There would now be less and less desultory journalism, less re-echoing of the only ideas he ever acquired — those of Flaubert — and an increasing relationship between his journalistic and his literary aims.   His stories would serve as newspaper contributions first and make books afterwards.

CHAPTER V

A BID FOR FAME

WHILE travelling in Algeria Maupassant called on Jules Lemaître, who had been appointed lecturer at the École Supérieure des Lettres at Algiers. Lemaître vaguely remembered having met him at Flaubert's, but he did recall the enthusiasm with which the Master had read "in a booming voice" one of Maupassant's poems. "I thought it wasn't bad; the mistrust aroused in me by the overflowing enthusiasm of old Flaubert prevented me from seeing that it was actually very good." Consequently, when Maupassant called, the rising critic had not troubled to read *Les Soirées de Médan*. "Someone had told me *Boule de Suif* was funny, and that sufficed." However, he politely inquired what M. de Maupassant was writing, and was told about a story of which the first scene was laid in a brothel and the second in a church. Lemaître nodded sagaciously and thought: "This fellow is obviously very pleased at having thought of such a contrast. How clever! I can see the thing already, half *Fille Élisa* and half *Faute de L'Abbé Mouret*. I don't think I'll bother about reading *you* until the weather gets cooler." And for three years Jules Lemaître lived quite happily without reading a line of Guy de Maupassant, whom everybody was praising.

Fortunately for him, *La Maison Tellier* found other readers and critics who were less indifferent. The copy of the *Figaro* which the officer in the desert had read, containing an article on Maupassant by Zola, was the issue of July 11, 1881, in which the new volume of stories was reviewed. "Maupassant has recently published *La Maison Tellier*, a collection of stories. I shall not dwell upon the title story, which is about the proprietress of a certain establishment who takes five women to the first communion of one of her nieces in a neighbouring village. The whole study centres upon the holiday of these girls, their youth which revives amidst the green fields, the religious emotion which overpowers them in the little chapel until their sobs reduce the whole congregation to tears. No analysis could be subtler, and the story will stand as a very curious psychological and physiological document, with the return of the women, happy, rejuvenated, perfumed by the balmy air of the country.

"People will say: 'Why choose such subjects? Could one not take respectable people?' Certainly, one could. But I think that Maupassant chose this subject because he felt its deep human note, stirring us to the depths. These unfortunates, kneeling in the chapel and sobbing, attracted him as a fine example of youthful education piercing through habits, however abominable; and also as showing the nerves of women, their need for romance, the faith which persists through their abject daily life. The author has not tried to make fun of religion, but rather to emphasize its power. It is a social and philosophical experiment, conducted both with audacity and discretion.

"Amongst the other stories in the book, those that I prefer are *Histoire d'une fille de ferme* and *En Famille*. I cannot analyse them at length. In the former a servant, after having a child by a ploughboy, marries her master, from whom she conceals the child, but who afterwards is happy to adopt it. In the second, a middle-class family pounces greedily on the inheritance of an old mother who has simply fallen into a lethargy, and whose resuscitation becomes a veritable thunderbolt. What I like in these stories is their fine simplicity. The *Histoire d'une fille de ferme*, particularly, opens with a grandiose, simple sweep. I advise those novelists who see our peasants through the eyes of Homer, or Shakespeare, or Hugo, to read these pages, where the right rural note is struck."

Maupassant had dedicated the book to Turgenev, who was responsible for the accurate reference to the English song which the disappointed sailors yelled outside Madame Tellier's house. "English sailors," he wrote, "sing 'Rule Britannia, Britannia rules the waves,' but you need only the first two words." Maupassant thus obtained the correct local colour for this passage: "The gentlemen were about to retire when the noisy band of men from the port reappeared at the end of the street. The French sailors were bawling the *Marseillaise* and the English *Rule Britannia*."

Unlike *Des Vers* and *Boule de Suif*, *La Maison Tellier* was not published by Charpentier, who never had any new work of Maupassant's after the latter was launched. This was all the more remarkable because Charpentier was not only the publisher of Flaubert, Daudet, Zola, Goncourt, Alexis, Huysmans, Hennique, and Céard, but he was also a great personal friend of the older and younger members of the Realistic and Naturalistic schools. His home was a centre for literary discussion, and his far-sighted generosity to Zola, which was eventually well rewarded, had endeared him to the group. Maupassant had complained to Flaubert about the stupidity of Mme. Charpentier, and he had apparently no wish to be associated with the firm. His choice was Victor Havard, who remained his publisher almost until his death, when all his books were transferred to the firm of Ollendorff, which issued the familiar squat volumes, with illustrations, now current.

Before sailing for North Africa, Maupassant had tried to see Havard, and he left three stories, receiving a letter which showed that his new publisher was a shrewd judge of what the public wanted. "I was very sorry to have been away when you called, but at last I have had the pleasure of reading the three stories you left for me. As you had given me to understand, *La Maison Tellier* is very audacious and startling. The subject is a dangerous one which, I believe, will arouse a great deal of anger and hypocritical indignation. However, it is saved by your talent and execution, and that is the main point. If I am not greatly mistaken, you will have a big success (I refer to sales, not to literary fame, which is already yours). As for *Le Papa de Simon*, it is absolutely a little masterpiece.

"As you expressed a keen desire to have this book sold as quickly as possible, I sent the three stories to the printer as soon as I had read them, and I should like you to be so kind as to make an appointment, so that we may decide upon the approximate date of publication. I hope that your indisposition has left no unpleasant results, and that you have completely recovered. I cannot allow you to fall ill now, for the time is most inopportune."

The reception of the volume justified Havard and was a relief to the author, who had not offered most of the contents to any periodical, because of the nature of the stories. *En Famille*, one of his most innocuous tales, had passed Mme. Adam intact, but *La Revue Politique et Littéraire* had done some violence to the relatively innocent text of *Histoire d'une fille de ferme*. A passage describing the operations of a cock amidst a lot of hens was suppressed completely, and a farmhand was permitted to walk up to the girl Rose, but not to place his hand upon her bosom. A reference to her approaching pregnancy was deleted, and the end of the story, explaining how the husband comes to accept his wife's illegitimate child, was arranged to suit a more conventional audience.

Having had this experience with a story at which even the most Anglo-Saxon cheek has never blushed, Maupassant must have seen the futility of offering such stories as *Une Partie de campagne* and *La Femme de Paul* to his editors. The contents of this volume, representing his free choice of subjects, unrestricted, and innocent of all editorial suggestion, are not without significance, apart from their merits of style and treatment. *Une Partie de campagne* describes the surrender of a mother and her daughter to two strangers, while her husband and prospective son-in-law are sleeping, after dining and drinking freely. *La Femme de Paul* is a tale of Lesbian love, in which a man drowns himself because his mistress is unfaithful to him with another woman. *Sur l'eau* is a story of alcoholic hallucination, the first of Maupassant's efforts to throw into narrative form the fears and nightmares of his waking and sleeping hours. A boat is anchored at night on the Seine; the anchor cannot be raised; a mist comes down; weird noises are heard and phantom figures approach; the hours of slow terror drag on; and when finally the boatman can get assistance the anchor is dragged up caught in the body of an old woman with a stone around her neck.

Le Papa de Simon is the author's conception of a simple story of sentiment, in which a poor little boy is tortured because he is a bastard and finally acquires a father when the honest village blacksmith marries his mother. *Au Printemps* is an effort to deal facetiously with the folly of men who are too susceptible to women.

A gloomy individual sees that a man has been attracted by a pretty girl, interrupts the flirtation, describes how he was trapped into marriage by yielding to a similar adventure, and prevents his listener from following the blonde charmer, who had, of course, "one of those smiles that madden."

Of the eight stories which Maupassant wrote for his first volume of collected prose, *La Maison Tellier* alone had the advantage of combining real observation and psychology with an original and ironical idea. But that idea was not his own; it was suggested by his old friend Charles Lapierre of Rouen, where Madame Tellier's establishment actually existed in the rue des Cordeliers. Hector Malot, of hallowed memory to schoolboy readers of *Sans Famille*, claimed that it was he who had told the anecdote, and he certainly added an improvement at the end, for in his version, as related to Toudouze at Maupassant's funeral, the ladies did not celebrate their return from the country: Mme. Tellier simply said: "To-night, you will go nicely to bye-bye alone."

Inventiveness and imagination are not the qualities which distinguish the volume, yet its success was considerable, twelve editions being sold in two years. Half of the stories were evocations of the author's life on the river, when Chatou and Maisons-Laffitte meant more to him than literary discussions. Here is La Grenouillère, the place of his youthful dreams, which he was so often to describe in one aspect or another:

"A crowd was strolling beneath the giant trees which made this corner of the island the most delicious park in the world. Women, girls with yellow hair, enormously rounded breasts, exaggerated hips, complexions plastered with rouge, made-up eyes, bright red lips, tightly laced, squeezed into extravagant dresses, exhibited the loud bad taste of their costumes as they dragged across the fresh lawns. At their sides young men posed in the clothes of tailor's dummies, with yellow gloves, patent leather boots, and canes as thin as wires, an eyeglass emphasizing the idiocy of their smiles. . . .

"In the floating restaurant there was a wild, shouting crowd. The wooden tables, where the spilled drinks made little sticky streams, were covered with half-emptied glasses and surrounded by half-intoxicated people. They all were shouting, singing, and bawling. Then men with red faces, their hats on the back of their heads, moved and shouted out of an animal impulse to make a noise. The women, on the lookout for their evening's prey, had themselves treated to drinks while waiting. The free space between the tables was given over to the usual frequenters of the place, a regiment of rowdy boating men with their girls in short flannel skirts. . . .

"In spite of the immense trees overshadowing the floating house, and in spite of the water all around, the heat in the place was suffocating. The smell of spilled liquor mixed with the odour of human bodies and with the violent perfumes in which the skin of the love-merchants is saturated, and which were evaporating in this oven. But beneath all these different odours there floated a light aroma of face powder, which disappeared at times but always returned, as if some invisible hand had shaken a hidden powder-puff in the air."

Une Partie de campagne, Maupassant once confided, was the record of his first adultery, and through it runs that suggestion of hectic physical desire peculiar to the early poems. It is assuredly a compatriot of Fragonard who thus modernized *L'Escarpolette*, in this picture of the girl in the swing:

"She was a pretty girl between eighteen and twenty years old, one of those women who spur one with a sudden desire on passing them in the street, and who leave

one with a vague uneasiness and an excitement of the
senses which last until evening. Tall, with a narrow
waist and wide hips, she had a very brown skin, very big
eyes, and very dark hair. Her dress clearly revealed the
firm plumpness of her body, which became more visible
because of the efforts she made to swing herself. Her
raised arms held the ropes above her head, so that her
breasts stood out, but did not quiver, each time she
shoved. Her hat, blown off by the wind, was lying behind her. Gradually the swing began to mount, and
each time it came down, it showed her slender legs right
up to the knees, and sent from her petticoats, into the
faces of the two men who laughingly watched her, a
breeze more intoxicating than the vapours of wine."

Already it was evident that whatever power Maupassant's writing had came to him through the stimulation
of two senses, one of which was the sense of vision.
Whatever he himself had seen, he could make others
see. And the one impulse which a woman could stir in
him, he could describe in a manner made vivid by the
intensity of his erotic imagination and the material
sharpness of his physical reactions. He could see anything and afterwards visualize it; he could feel only one
thing intensely, and with phrases which became in
time almost stereotyped, he tried to convey that feeling.
Thus the young lady in *Au Printemps:*

"She had the grace of the typical Parisienne, an
adorable blond head with curls over her temples; hair
that looked like curled light came down to her ears,
reached her neck, danced in the wind, and then became,
lower down, such a fine, light, blond fluff that it was
scarcely visible, but aroused an irresistible desire to
plant kisses there."

The repetition throughout Maupassant's work of similar references to rebellious blond curls, to hair falling

seductively over the forehead, the temples, the neck, and the ears, to kisses on the soft down behind the ears and on the nape of the neck, "where the perfume of the body rises," became so definite a series of formulæ that they could be tabulated: a German physiognomist finally arriving at the statistical fact that the dark-haired Maupassant preferred blond women, ninety-three of his heroines being blondes, eleven brunette, seventeen black-haired, and six red-haired — in inverse ratio to the distribution of those colours in France!

In order to satisfy the demand which *La Maison Tellier* had created Maupassant began more regularly to contribute stories to the periodicals over the name of "Maufrigneuse," and very soon he had another volume ready, consisting chiefly of reprinted stories, although the title story, *Mlle. Fifi*, had not been published elsewhere when Henry Kistemaeckers of Brussels issued the handsome little book in June 1882, with an etched portrait by Just as a frontispiece. This edition, which contained only seven stories, was exhausted in a few days, and by the time Havard republished it, the following year, the volume contained eleven additional stories.

Henry Kistemaeckers was at this time a prominent publisher of books which, on political or moral grounds, could not be published in France. He had lost money as the publisher of radical works by the exiled intellectuals of the Paris Commune, so he turned his enthusiasm to the Naturalist movement, and became sponsor for all the lewd and wicked works, both ancient and modern, which Marshall MacMahon and Casimir Périer wished to prohibit in France. In the seventies even Casanova was contraband and was smuggled in over the Belgian frontier, together with Kistemaeckers' other classics, Faublas, Alexandre Nerciat, Restif de la Bretonne, and the rest.

Kistemaeckers, who made beautiful books, and had the assistance of artists like Rops, was constantly in conflict with the authorities, but he secured more acquittals than any other publisher, before or since — eighteen prosecutions and eighteen acquittals at the Cour d'Assises, and only two adverse judgments out of five in the lower courts, all within the space of a few years. Finally he was condemned in 1902 for the advertisements on the fourth page of *Le Flirt*, that more nude and lascivious predecessor of the papers which the Great War brought into every Anglo-Saxon home. He fled to France, where, in 1905, the authorities refused to extradite him, and where he now lives, in the neighbourhood of Paris, surrounded by drawings of Steinlen, Rops, and Willette, and the three hundred books which he issued during his thirty years of publishing.

Huysmans was the link between the Belgian publisher and his friends in Paris, for he had published his first novel, *Marthe*, with Gay of Brussels in 1876, and in 1879 he wrote an introduction to *Rimes de Joie*, by Théodore Hannon, the editor of *L'Artiste*, in which *Sac-au-Dos* and Céard's novel, *Une Belle journée*, had first appeared. In 1881 Kistemaeckers reissued Hannon's book, thus establishing relations with the Médan group, and that year Léon Hennique gave him a volume of stories. In 1882, when Maupassant went to him, Kistemaeckers also issued *A vau-l'eau*, by Huysmans, Edouard Rod's *La Chute de Miss Topsy*, and *Le Mort*, by Camille Lemonnier, Zola's greatest disciple in Belgium, whose famous novel *Un Mâle* he had already published. Paul Alexis naturally followed with *Le Collage*, and Maupassant's friend Harry Alis, who had accompanied him to Algeria, produced *Les Pas-de-Chance*. Then Henry Céard wrote a preface to Paul Bonnetain's *Charlot s'amuse*, which was not, as certain American movie "æstheti-

cians " might imagine, Charlie Chaplin in an earlier
incarnation, for, contrary to their superstition, Charlot
is not a mystic projection of Mr. Chaplin's personality,
but a common French abbreviation, in this case, of a
Charles whose onanism provided the subject of a typical
novel of this period. The book gave rise to one of the
most famous trials in the history of Naturalism, but
Bonnetain contented himself with Zola's retort: "I have
written a scientific work "; and the jury believed him!

Kistemaeckers was afterwards heard to admit that
Bonnetain was not sincere, and he complained that
Alexis was never satisfied. Maupassant, on the other
hand, "was the best fellow in the world. We often used
to dine together when he lived in the rue des Dames.
One evening, after I had gone to meet him at the offices
of *Gil Blas*, he introduced me, on the boulevard, to Paul
Hervieu, who had just pubished *Diogène-le-chien*. Maupassant decided to take us home to dinner, so we went
to buy some provisions. We bought wine, a jar of foie
gras, and a cold fowl. But suddenly Maupassant
stopped on the pavement: 'Oh, my God!' he exclaimed,
'I was forgetting. I have a woman dining with me!'
And, making the best excuses he could, he ran off to his
rendez-vous with his arms full of provisions."

That summer of 1882, when Charpentier published
Hervieu's first novel, Maupassant greeted the newcomer in *Gil Blas*, but soon in *Le Gaulois* he was again
writing an apologia for Naturalism. He had again
profited by the particular attention which that school
invariably aroused, and the mere sight of the Kistemaeckers imprint, for which he had momentarily for-
saken Havard, was like a red rag to the critical bulls. A
new law against pornographic literature had been
passed, and it was the text of Francisque Sarcey's discourse on the 4th of July in *Le XIXe Siècle:*

"I regret the tendency which seems nowadays to drive young men of incontestable merit to unpleasant subjects. . . . Even courtesans no longer attract them; they affect some strange taste for the common prostitute, licensed or in brothels. Here, for example, is M. Guy de Maupassant, a young writer of the greatest talent. He can see and he can tell a story. . . . Yet, it is inexplicable to me why he persists in coming back to this ugly subject in every volume he publishes. Why take so much trouble to study creatures so unworthy of interest? These depraved souls are capable of not more than a few sentiments, all of an animal nature. They are so quickly exhausted, and it is in vain that the author arms himself with a penetrating analysis: you cannot draw blood from a stone. . . .

"On reading *La Maison Tellier*, I could not help saying: 'What a fine style so badly wasted!' And this time we get *Mlle. Fifi*. Another story of the same type! . . . Is it not high time for M. Guy de Maupassant to turn his powers of observation and his gift of style to some other subjects? I warn him that the public is beginning to grow very tired of these ugly scenes. It is not the courts which will fine or imprison him. . . . The judgment which M. Guy de Maupassant has to fear is infinitely more serious."

Albert Wolff, of *Le Figaro*, forgetting his judgment of two years earlier, that, save Zola's, the stories in *Les Soirées de Médan* were "the last word in mediocrity," announced himself as a pained admirer, who felt it his duty, however unpleasant, to remonstrate:

"Amongst the new novelists there is none whom I like as much as M. Guy de Maupassant; none of them irritates me as much as he. . . . All the younger writers have one prejudice in common: they call it studying the lower depths of society. . . . For a man of talent like M. de Maupassant, there can be neither honour nor profit in adding to the already considerable regiment of these literary sewer-cleaners. . . . Take it from me, M. de Maupassant, it is unnecessary to take one's pen always into brothels in order to prove one's talent."

Maupassant replied to Sarcey with a preliminary expression of thanks for his kind words and a regret that he should be personally involved in a discussion which was of general rather than particular interest. "Ever since literature has existed," he went on, "writers have always energetically demanded the greatest freedom in the choice of their subjects. Victor Hugo, Gautier, Flaubert, and many others have been rightly irritated by the claim of critics to impose a particular kind of literature upon the novelists. One might as well reproach prose writers with not being poets, idealists with not being realists, etc.

"An author is and must remain his own master, the sole judge of what he feels capable of writing. It is for the critics, for his colleagues, for the public to decide whether he has accomplished his task well or ill. The reader can pass judgment upon the execution. If I am prompted to criticize or to contest a man's talent, I cannot do it unless I look at it from his point of view and understand his secret intentions. I have no right to accuse M. Feuillet of never having anything to say about the working-class, or M. Zola of never choosing virtuous people. It does not follow that we may not retain our preferences for certain ideas and subjects.

"Here we come to the most debated question of the last ten years. I cannot do better, it seems to me, than begin by quoting a passage from a very remarkable letter of M. Taine's, whose view I do not share, and which coincides, moreover, with that of M. Francisque Sarcey:

"'In the second rôle all that remains for me is to beg you to add to your observations another series of observations. You describe peasants, people of the lower middle class, workmen, students, and prostitutes. No doubt you will some day describe the cultured class, the upper middle-class, engineers, doctors, professors, industrial magnates, and merchants.

"'In my view civilization is a power. A man born in easy circumstances, the descendant of three or four respectable generations, has more chances of being honest, refined, and educated. Honour and intelligence are always hot-house plants, more or less. This doctrine is very aristocratic, but it is experimental. . . .'

"Add to this the wish formulated by a masterly novelist, Edmond de Goncourt, to see the young writers applying to society, to real society, the methods of scrupulous observation which writers have long been applying to the analysis of the lower classes. And now let us wonder why men of letters always neglect the people who alone seem interesting to study. Why? Is it, as Edmond de Goncourt says, because it is infinitely more difficult to read into those hearts and souls and intentions? Perhaps; to some extent. But there is another reason.

"The modern novelist tries chiefly to catch humanity in the act. What interests him, therefore, is first to discover in every human action the initial motive, the mysterious origin of the wish, and especially the determining factors common to the whole race, the instinctive impulses. Now, what principally distinguishes people in society from simpler individuals is mainly a sort of veneer of conventions, a layer of complicated hypocrisy.

"Consequently, the novelist finds himself faced with this alternative: either to describe the world as he sees it, to raise the veils of decency and respectability, to show what exists underneath the outward appearance, to show human beings always alike despite their borrowed trappings, or to decide to create an ideal and charming world, as George Sand, Jules Sandeau, and Octave Feuillet have done. Not that one should attack and condemn this decision to describe only the pleasant exterior and the attractive surface. But when an author is endowed with a temperament which permits him to express only what he believes to be the truth, he cannot be compelled to deceive consciously both himself and others.

"M. Francisque Sarcey is astonished and irritated because courtesans and strumpets have been invading our literature for the last forty years, and have monopolized the novel and the play. I might reply by citing *Manon Lescaut* and all the spicy literature of the end of the last century. But quotations are never conclusive. The real reason is surely this: literature is never concerned with exact observation. Now, woman has two functions in this life: love and maternity. The novelists, perhaps wrongly, have always regarded the former of these two functions as being more interesting to their readers than the second, and they have, first of all, studied woman in the exercise of the profession for which she seemed born. Of all subjects, love touches the public most. We have been particularly interested in the woman made for love.

"Further, there are profound differences of intelligence amongst men, the result of education, environment, and so forth. With woman it is not so. Her rôle in life is restricted; her faculties remain limited; from top to bottom of the social scale she remains identical. Women of easy virtue become remarkable women of the world in a short time, once they are married. They

adapt themselves to their environment. A proverb says
that a cat may look at a king. Every day we rub elbows
with cats, or even worse than that, who have become
ladies and hold their place in society like others.

"Women are not divided into classes. They have a
place in society solely because of the men who marry
them or push them. Are men always so scrupulous
about a woman's origins when they take her as a companion, legitimate or otherwise? Must we be more so
when we take them as literary subjects?

"M. Taine said in his letter that honour and intelligence were hot-house plants, more or less. So far as
intelligence is concerned, I agree. But what about
honour? . . . I remember this question was being discussed one day in the presence of a young lady from the
provinces, but of the best society, an aristocrat to her
finger-tips. She became irritated at hearing that right
and noble feelings were commoner amongst the middle
than the upper classes. Then, when examples were being quoted, she suddenly began to laugh and agreed
that we were not altogether wrong; not altogether. She
had remembered something. Just after the war of 1870
she was asked by a committee to collect money to lib-
erate the district, in the large manufacturing town where
she lived. She began with the poorer quarters. She
met, of course, people who were brutes, but she also
found many poor devils who sacrificed their dinner
money. Women of the people, deeply touched, tried to
kiss her, and the men, as they offered their *sous*,
squeezed her hands until they hurt her. When she
reached the middle-class quarters, she was told the master and mistress were out, or, if she caught them at
home, they cheated in order to give less, making hypocritical excuses; behaving like cads, for all their fine
phrases.

trains; the sea swallows them up; chimneys fall on pedestrians when there is a storm. But what novelist of the new school would dare, in the middle of a story, to eliminate one of his chief characters by means of an unforeseen accident of this kind?

"Considering the life of every man as a novel, every time a man dies in this way, nature has suddenly interrupted a novel. In each case we have no right to copy nature, for we must always take what is the average and general. Therefore, to see in humanity one class of people (whether it be the upper or the lower class), one category of feelings, one order of events, is assuredly an indication of narrow-mindedness, a sign of intellectual myopia. Balzac, whom we all quote, irrespective of our tendencies, because his mind was as varied as it was broad, Balzac considered humanity as a whole, facts in masses, and he catalogued in huge series of human beings and human passions. If we seem to abuse the microscope nowadays, and always to study the same human insect, it is our loss. It is because we are powerless to show ourselves on a vaster scale. But let us rest assured that the present school of literature will certainly extend the limits of its studies by degrees, and will get rid of all prejudices.

"On closer observation the persistent reproduction of the 'lower depths' is in reality merely a protest against the immemorial theory of things poetic. All sentimental literature has lived indefinitely on this belief that there existed certain sentiments, certain things, which were essentially noble and poetic, and that only these could furnish the writer with subjects. For centuries the poets sang only of young girls, stars, springtime, and flowers. In the drama even evil passions, hate, and jealousy were exalted and magnificent.

"To-day we laugh at the songs about the dew, and we

have learnt that every action in life, that all things have an equal interest in art. But, as soon as this truth was discovered, the writers, in a spirit of reaction, have perhaps become too obstinately preoccupied with the opposite of what used to be celebrated. Once this crisis is over, and it must come to an end, the novelists will see with an accurate eye and a fair mind all sorts of people and facts, and, according to their talent, their works will include as much as possible of life in all its manifestations.

"It is precisely in order to clear away literary prejudices that others have been created which are quite the contrary of the first. In short, if there is one motto which the modern novelist should adopt, a motto which sums up in a few words what he is trying to do, is it not this: 'I strive that nothing human may be alien to me'?"

Thus the pornographic aura of Kistemaeckers enveloped a little book with whose contents it is otherwise difficult to reconcile these solemn debates. The seven stories were not particularly concerned with low life. In *Mlle. Fifi* the patriotism of Rachel earned for her a respectable husband, and, unlike Boule de Suif, she did not make a sacrifice of her virtue to the Prussian officer. The title of the story has so frequently caused it to be confused with *Boule de Suif* that one suspects much of the denunciation to have been due to such confusion, for it requires a stretch of imagination to see in a melodramatic Prussian War story a continued preoccupation with the ladies of Madame Tellier's profession. The only other story which had not been published in periodical form, *Un Réveillon*, is one of the author's characteristic pieces of sardonic humour, in which the corpse of a grandfather is consigned to the food bin which the family uses as a table to celebrate their Christmas feast.

Between December 1881 and March 1882, Maupassant had published five of the stories, and by the following February, when the enlarged edition was delivered to Havard, some fifty more stories had appeared in the *Gaulois* and *Gil Blas* in addition to the numerous articles which have never been collected. It was a period of intensive productivity, as his posthumous works showed, but he rejected fourteen of these stories when preparing the edition of *Mlle. Fifi* which Havard published in 1883. Had Uncle Sarcey been confronted with an apology for incest, such as *M. Jocaste*, he might have protested, and he would probably have seen in *La Farce*, with its joke about an explosive powder in a certain chamber utensil, nothing more than a charming expression of Gallic wit. As it was, these tales lay with many others until Madame Laure de Maupassant surrendered her son's uncollected writings to his publisher.

Inferior as many of them were, they compare favourably, for the most part, with the average story which Maupassant deemed worthy of his volumes. The feebleness and bad taste of such things as *Mots d'Amour*, which appears in both editions of *Mlle. Fifi*, make one wonder what could have been the defects in the ten contemporary pieces which caused them to be passed over, even when three different publishers in addition to Havard were issuing this prodigious output of stories in book form. Rouveyre and Bloud received sixteen for the volume *Contes de la Bécasse* in the spring of 1883; by the autumn twelve more were ready for Monnier's edition of *Clair de lune;* and when the year ended there was enough material to complete *Les Sœurs Rondoli* for Ollendorff, and *Miss Harriet* for Havard.

All of Maupassant's qualities, his good and bad characteristics, were present in the work which flowed in a full and steady stream during these two years of amazing fecundity. When Anatole France greeted him as a writer of modern *fabliaux,* that peculiarly French creation, he expressed the pleasure which French readers experienced in the presence of an author whose lineage went back to the thirteenth century. *La Légende du Mont-Saint-Michel* was a definite attempt to relate an old legend in the form in which it survived as a Norman folk tale. Naïve peasant humour, the source of many of his tales, was illustrated in *L'Ane, Farce Normande,* and *Le Remplaçant,* where the material in itself is slight: by trickery a dead donkey is sold as valuable game; a bridegroom is called out on his wedding night and is prevented from attending to duties more pleasant than chasing imaginary poachers; in certain amorous affairs two lovers are better than one. *Rencontre* relates how a husband who is separated from his wife can be used to make an honest woman of her, and *Décoré* is a variation upon the time-honoured theme of cuckoldry, showing how a husband's forehead is adorned simultaneously with his buttonhole. *Le mal d'André* demonstrates that a resourceful lover can overcome even so formidable an obstacle as the presence of an innocent child on the nuptial couch. The subjects and their treatment are in the authentic tradition of the medieval farce.

Some of Maupassant's most famous stories belong to this first abundant harvest. In addition to *Boule de Suif, Mlle. Fifi,* and *La Maison Tellier* came *Ce cochon de Morin, La Ficelle, Les Bijoux,* and *L'Heritage.* Here the fabliau is the kernel, but a greater or lesser degree of elaboration and sophistication transformed them into the kind of story with which the author's name was to be universally identified. His skill in expanding an anecdote or a whimsical joke was illustrated in *Le pain maudit,* which English and American readers will recognize as closely allied to the song:

In a little country village,
Where her aged parents live,
They drink the champagne that she sends them,
But they never will forgive.

Charles Lapierre, to whom he owed the story of *La
Maison Tellier*, also gave him the situation for *Ce cochon
de Morin*, Lapierre having actually played the part of
the friend who succeeds with the damsel whose virtue
was the cause of Morin's undoing.

La Ficelle was a perfect specimen of that improvement upon the Naturalistic formula for a story in which
nothing happens, which Maupassant made his own. He
takes the same kind of unimportant fact, the same
simple sequence of everyday incidents, but in the end
they lead to a miniature drama as inevitable in its doom
as a Greek tragedy. If Maître Hauchecorne had not
picked up a piece of string, he would have been a less
economical but a wiser Norman. *À cheval* also showed
the dire consequences produced by an innocent escapade.

L'Heritage, the most elaborate of these stories in its
final form (as published in *Miss Harriet*), shows the
author's method of developing an idea. On its first appearance as *Un million*, in 1882, it was about one fifth
of the length, and was simply a baldly cynical story,
comparable to *Le pain maudit*, of a sterile husband who
allows his wife to have a child by another man in order
to inherit a fortune. Expanded to a length of more than
one hundred pages, it was transformed into a realistic
study of the life of a minor Civil Servant, drawn from
Maupassant's experience at the Ministry of Marine. In
the detailed setting of this bourgeois existence the original story becomes a *leitmotiv*, and the attitude of each
person is determined by the rise and fall of the hopes
centred upon the birth of the child. When it is decided

to invoke outside help in order to bring about the consummation which all so devoutly wish, the different points of view of the husband, the wife, the lover, and the family are indicated by masterly strokes, not the least of which is the elimination of the lover once he has discharged successfully the function for which he was selected. The apotheosis of the virtuous wife and happy mother becomes, in the end, not an amusing cynicism, but a genuine piece of ironical psychology.

While these stories, with their virtues and their weaknesses, at once explain Maupassant's immediate success, we can look to them for more than the varied qualities which give the measure of his talent. They also throw a light upon his own condition when he returned from Africa, after that attack of melancholia so unexpected in a young author rising on the wave of great popular success. In *Marroca* he wrote a footnote to his Algerian experiences, which has a familiar ring: "Here people love madly. During the very first days one feels a thrilling ardour, a stimulation, a sudden tension of desire, a tingling right down to the finger-tips, which excite one's sexual powers, and all one's faculties of physical sensation, to the point of exasperation, from the merest touching of hands to that craving, that shall be nameless, which makes us do so many foolish things. . . . I do not know whether what you call love of the heart, love of the soul, whether sentimental idealism, platonic love, in brief, can exist in this world. I doubt it. But the other kind of love, the love of the senses, which is good, very good, indeed, is really terrible in this climate."

Marroca, the daughter of Spanish colonists, supplies a story to illustrate what might be expected from Maupassant under such conditions. "She was truly a wonderful girl, of a rather animal type, but superb. Her eyes always seemed to be shining with passion; her half-opened mouth, her sharp teeth, even her smile, had something atrociously sensual about them; and her strange breasts, long and straight, with points like pears of flesh, as elastic as if steel springs were concealed in them . . . made of her a creature destined for riotous love. . . . No woman's body ever burned with such insatiable desires." Of course every effort is made to do justice to so charming a creature, who was prepared to kill her husband with a hatchet had he interfered. And with a vaudeville bow Maupassant concludes: "That, my dear man, is the way conjugal duty, love, and hospitality are understood here." Even as late as 1889 this memory was still vivid, and *Allouma* again recorded in a similar setting "the eternal struggle between two human animals, the male and the female, in which the male is always vanquished." Again the breasts are "long and pointed, and as supple as though on springs," but now a distinction is drawn. "I did not love her — no — one does not love the women of this primitive continent. . . . They have too rudimentary a heart, their sensitiveness is not refined enough to awaken in our souls that sentimental exaltation which is the poetry of love."

The difference is one of mood, not of taste, and to that difference factors great and small had curiously contributed. With a diminution of physical health came a softening of sentiment, but mental ill-health did not correspond to any weakening of the erotic imagination, because the two were closely allied and largely dependent one upon the other. Of that unhealthy mind there was a glimpse in *Mlle. Fifi*, when the story *Fou?* raised its question mark against a man whose jealousy of his mistress prompts him to kill her horse because he has seen signs of sexual satisfaction in her pleasure in riding the animal. In *Apparition* Maupassant's voice is audible in the middle of a not very brilliant ghost-story: "I do not believe in ghosts, but I have almost fainted in fear of the dead. I have suffered, oh, how I have suffered, more in a few moments than in the entire rest of my life from the unconquerable anguish of super-natural terrors."

Suicides contains a confession which is curiously akin to the declaration of misery which accompanies *Au Soleil:* "For some years now something has been happening to me. All the events of life which once were as resplendent in my eyes as the dawn seem to be growing pale. The significance of things has been revealed to me in its brutal reality, and the real reason for love has disgusted me for ever with poetic tenderness. We are the eternal playthings of stupid and charming illusions that never die. . . . Once I was happy. Everything was charming: the women passing, the appearance of the street, the place where I live. I was interested even in the cut of clothes. But the repetition of the same sights finally filled my heart with lassitude and boredom, as it would a play-goer who went every night to the same theatre. Every day for thirty years I have been getting up at the same hour, and for thirty years at the same restaurant I have been eating at the same hours the same dishes served by different waiters. I have tried travelling. The isolation which one feels in unfamiliar places frightened me. I felt so terribly alone in the world, and so small, that I quickly returned home. But then the unchanging physiognomy of my furniture, in the same place for thirty years . . . sickened me of habits and of the black gloom of living in such a way. . . .

"Every day, when shaving, I have a great desire to cut my throat. Several times my face, which never

changes, reflected in the little glass, with soap on my
cheeks, has made me weep from sadness. I cannot even
enjoy any more the society of the people whom I used
to like meeting. I know them so well, what they will
say, what I shall reply. I have so often seen the un-
alterable mould of their thoughts, the line of their
arguments. Every brain is a circus in which a poor
imprisoned horse runs round and round. Whatever our
efforts, our twists and turns, the boundary is near,
rounded continuously, without any unexpected uneven-
ness, without any gate leading to the unknown. We
must keep continually turning around the same ideas,
the same joys, the same jokes, the same habits, the
same beliefs, the same disgusts."

With a thought for his mother and for some women he
loved, the hero of these melancholy reflections shoots
himself. Even in the spring of 1883 Guy de Maupassant
is not gay. In July he told the story, for the first time,
of what was haunting him, and *Lui?* seemed to some a
curious story of hallucination, and to others it suggested
a parallel with Musset's *Nuit de décembre*. But there
was a vast difference between the simple fantasy of that
poet, even if his visions were due to alcohol, and the
remarkable case of autoscopy which Maupassant described.

Once again an unkind fate threw a shadow over his
life when all seemed well. In 1880 Flaubert had died,
just when Maupassant was making his remarkable *début*. In 1883 he was in full possession of all his creative
faculties, and he was working at such a pitch that his
output of stories up to the end of that year was nearly
half the total number which he produced during the
whole ten years of his active literary career. As late as
1888 his volumes were still drawing, at least in part,
upon the stories of that much earlier year for material.

Yet there were twenty-two stories belonging to this period unreprinted during his lifetime, enough to make a stouter volume than usual. Four of them, it is true, were preliminary sketches for the two novels upon which he was also engaged, as if to show that his capacity was unlimited. *Par un soir de printemps* in May 1881, *Les aut du berger* in March, and *La Veillée* in June 1882, were the first seeds of *Une Vie*, and in November 1883 *Le Vengeur* showed he was working at *Bel-Ami*.

That same month he acquired his valet François of literary memory, and he was in possession of his own villa, La Guillette at Étretat. He had made a strenuous and honourable bid for fame, and fame had come to him, bearing gifts of money which satisfied the Norman in him, and the literary appreciation of his compeers, which gratified the adopted son of Flaubert. But his joy in all these things was diminished, and they were soon to lose all their savour, because they were accompanied by the first intimations of insanity — for such is the retrospective diagnosis of conditions about which even Maupassant himself felt unhappy, though with what degree of ignorance of the real facts it is hard, at this point, to say.

CHAPTER VI

THE METEOR

AUPASSANT had worked very hard at his first novel, *Une Vie*, which ran serially in *Gil Blas* from the end of February to the beginning of April, 1883, and was issued immediately afterwards by Havard. He had nearly completed and had then laid aside an earlier version of the story, of which the frequently corrected manuscript survives to illustrate the sure sense of self-criticism which led him to recast and rewrite the whole novel, eliminating all repetition, strengthening the outline, at first a little vague, and polishing and sharpening his phrases with something of Flaubert's conscientiousness. The book at once met with popular success, and the author began to feel that he was justified in aiming higher than he had done in his innumerable short stories of such varying merit.

The faithful Alexis, of course, was early in the field with a laudatory review. "This book is life itself, the common events of every day. It touches the heart because it is human. All women will believe, more or less, that they are Jeanne, will recognize their own emotions and will be particularly touched. . . . The general effect is powerful and the style carries everything before it. . . ." The *Temps* was still troubled about Maupassant's pessimism, "the pessimism which prevented Flaubert from renewing himself and has smitten Zola with psychological impotence." But the praise was not grudging and was sound. "M. de Maupassant chooses his words; he does not affect them. He is content if they are the right words with which to secure a sonorous phrase or harmonious colouring. This fine simplicity, so sure of itself, lends a great charm to his descriptions; a few characteristic traits, vividly observed and powerfully expressed, suffice for him. . . ."

After due reflection even Brunetière unbent in the pontifical pages of the *Revue des Deux Mondes*. Maupassant had all the faults of the Naturalist school, but also certain qualities, which were noticeable in *Une Vie*. "Like Flaubert, he is chiefly lacking in taste and restraint. But for that, and for certain pages which look like a challenge, *Une Vie* would almost be a remarkable work. It is certainly a very simple, very banal story, but it is readable. As I wanted to discuss it, I found I could read it without being bored." A minor academic bleat was heard in *La Revue Bleue*, where *Une Vie* was taken as a sign that realism was forsaking "the slum and the gutter," and it was admitted that "the principal characters are drawn by the hand of a master and stand out in bold relief . . . the work of a remarkable stylist and colourist." Finally *Le Figaro*, making amends for Albert Wolff's previous performances, allowed Philippe Gille to say that "the author has taken a great step forward and reached sufficiently high ground for his personality to be clearly visible. Having begun as a pupil of Zola, M. de Maupassant has now left school." Nevertheless, the book was not sold by the railway station news-agents, on the ground that it was immoral.

Although the novel had been in his mind for several years and he had been working at it since 1881, *Une Vie* was completely dissociated from his actual life and experiences during the years when it was written, for Paris is entirely absent from its pages. The book was the final chapter of his existence as a young man at Étretat,

the summary of a life which he had left behind him, and
which he evokes with a plenitude of detail, a sense of
affectionate possession, as a Norman who alone can
know his own people and feel with them.   He drew
plentifully upon his memories, and even the initial idea,
the disillusionment of a woman, first as a wife and then
as a mother, was suggested by the domestic difficulties
of his own parents.   He described the family house under the name of Les Peuples, and as every aspect of the
countryside was impressed upon his imagination from
childhood, he could draw a series of ever-changing pictures in which the tang of earth and fresh sea-breezes
is felt, the dreary winters and glorious summers, the
lives of folk who are half peasants and half fishermen.
An overpowering sense of reality pervades *Une Vie*, a
feeling that all these events have actually happened,
that a life, not a story, has been unfolded.   Nominally,
it is the existence of one woman which is related, but
the effect is to transcend the life of a woman and to
show us the life of man, the futility of all human dreams.

The disillusionment is not a new note in Maupassant,
but what is new and unique in this first novel is its freedom from the author's usual obsessions.   It almost
seems as if the elimination of Paris from his imagination
automatically released him from his eternal preoccupation, personal and general, with the purely sexual con-
flicts of men and women.   The Parisian *chroniqueur* is
possibly responsible for the not altogether necessary
scene of Jeanne's discovery of her mother's adultery, for
the incident of the old love-letters had been used by
"Maufrigneuse" in *Le Gaulois*, but there is very
little "Maufrigneuserie" in *Une Vie*, for the two other
fragments similarly published, the story of Tante Lison,
and the driving of the caravan, in which the lovers are
imprisoned, down the hill and over the cliff on to the

seashore, are not exactly in the "Maufrigneuse" manner. When a real story, when situations having their
roots in the realities of human existence, possessed him,
Maupassant could forget about the perfume of women,
about the humours of prostitution, and about the endless trivialities and superficialities which supplied him
with the necessary anecdotes. *Une Vie* was the record of
the only period in his career when he was in close contact with normal life, and it is the most solid and universal of all his writings.

Francisque Sarcey gave the book his blessing, and an
Englishman, John Eggers, was allowed to make the
first translation of Maupassant, when he paid five hundred francs for the privilege of offering *A Woman's Life*
to the British public. The book was published in London in 1885, and was followed by *Bel-Ami*, both of
which were used as evidence of Vizetelly and Company's
evil intentions, when the firm was prosecuted for publishing the works of Zola in 1888. Meanwhile, despite
a bad publishing season, Havard reported that the sales
were "pretty good," although the year 1883 was one of
commercial depression in France and the earlier volumes
did not do so well. That spring there was trouble in
Cochin-China, and Lieutenant Viaud, whose *Mariage
de Loti* and *Roman d'un Spahi* had been rival stars on
the literary horizon, departed for Tonkin, whence he
sent to *Le Figaro* such descriptions of butchery amongst
the Annamites by French sailors that he was recalled,
but he protested his innocence so fervently that literary
candour, not anti-militarism, was the only charge that
stood against him. Oscar Wilde dined with Edmond de
Goncourt and told him that in Texas real criminals were
sought to play the parts of villains in the theatre, and
that "ten years' hard labour" was mentioned after
the name of a poisoner who filled the rôle of Lady Mac-

beth, as her title to the distinction. At the Charpen-
tiers' one evening, after dinner, the remnant of the
"Five" deplored "the absence of enthusiasm, gaiety,
and youth" in the rising young authors, Goncourt opin-
ing that young people cannot be otherwise than sad "in
a country without glory, where the cost of living is high."

Neither glory nor money with which to meet the high
cost of living was lacking to Maupassant now. His
mother had ceded a piece of land to him at one end of
Étretat and he had built a little house on it, and rapidly
he was transforming it into a comfortable two-storey
cottage, building a projecting wing at each end connected by a wooden balcony. The walls were of yellow
plaster and the roof of red tiles, all covered with twining
creepers. The property was bordered by ash and poplar
trees and, according to season, the beds in the garden
bloomed with roses and carnations, dahlias or chrysan-
themums. An overturned boat, lying on its side upon
brick pillars, surrounded by a privet hedge, served as a
bathroom and as the valet's bedroom. In the apple-
orchard was a pond filled with goldfish especially im-
ported from Japan. There were strawberry beds, a
croquet lawn, and a rifle-range. Poultry, several dogs,
two cats, a monkey, and a parrot — who greeted the
ladies with "*Bonjour, petite cochonne!*" — completed
the charm of La Guillette, which Maupassant wanted
to call "La Maison Tellier," but was dissuaded by his
more sensitive visitors of the sex most concerned in this
witticism. By the summer of 1883 it was ready to receive the author and his friends, and he spent a part of
each year there during a considerable period of his life.
It was his refuge in order to work, and also his play-
ground in summer.

Before going down to Étretat that first summer, Maupassant confessed that he felt more and more incapable

*La Guillette, Maupassant's country house -
at Etretat*

of loving one woman because he loved all the others too well. "I should like to have a thousand arms, a thousand lips, and thousand . . . temperaments, in order to embrace at one time an army of these charming and unimportant creatures." But he also made a confession which came strangely after this heartfelt cry, for, as it turned out, that confession was the pathological result of the previous avowal. He confessed that he was beginning to dread being alone. But that fear was not yet so mortal as it subsequently became. He could still speak of it with a degree of detachment, and so he cast his confession into the form of a story about a man who was getting married in order not to be alone at night.

"I am not afraid of danger. If a man were to enter, I should kill him without a tremor. I am not afraid of ghosts; I do not believe in the supernatural, I am not afraid of the dead; I believe in the definite annihilation of every human being that dies. . . . But I am afraid of myself. I am afraid of fear, afraid of the spasms of my terrorized mind, afraid of the horrible sensation of incomprehensible fear. . . . It is awful, incurable. I am afraid of the walls, of the furniture, of the familiar objects which take on a sort of animal life in my sight. Above all I am frightened by the disturbance of my mind, of my reason which slips away from me, all blurred, scattered by a mysterious and invisible terror.

"At first I feel a vague uneasiness stealing into my mind, which makes me shiver. I look around. Nothing! And I expect something! What? Something comprehensible, since I am frightened solely because I do not understand my fear. I speak! I am afraid of my own voice. I walk! I am afraid of something unknown behind the door, behind the curtain, in the wardrobe, under the bed. Yet I know that there is nothing anywhere. I turn around suddenly because I am afraid of what is behind me, although there is nothing and I know it. I move, and feel my terror increasing. I shut myself in my room, bury myself in my bed, and hide under the sheets. Rolled up in a ball, I shut my eyes in desperation, and I remain like that for an infinite space of time, remembering that my lighted candle is on the night table and it must be extinguished. Yet I dare not do it. . . .

"Once upon a time I felt nothing of the kind. I came home quietly. I came and went in my flat, and nothing troubled the serenity of my mind. Had anyone told me what incredible, stupid, and terrible illness of fear would one day afflict me, I should have laughed. I used to open the doors in the darkness with confidence; I went slowly to bed without pushing the bolts in the locks, and I never got up in the middle of the night to see that all means of access to my room were properly closed. It all began in a curious way last year.

"It was a damp evening in autumn. When the servant had left me after dinner, I began to wonder what I should do. For a while I walked up and down my room. I felt tired, oppressed for some reason, unable to work, or even to read. A fine rain streamed down the windows. I was depressed, overpowered by one of those fits of sadness which make one want to cry, to talk to anybody in order to shake off the weight of one's thoughts.

"I felt lonely, my rooms seemed empty as they never had been before. An infinite and heartbreaking solitude surrounded me. What should I do? I sat down. Then a nervous impatience ran through my legs. I got up and began to walk again. Perhaps I also had a touch of fever, for I noticed that my hands, which I held behind my back, as one often does when walking slowly, were burning each other. Then I suddenly felt a cold chill down my spine. I fancied the damp outside had got into the house, and I thought of lighting the fire. I lit it, for the first time that year. Then I sat down again and watched the flames. But soon the impossibility of remaining still made me get up again, and I felt I should have to go out, to shake myself, to look up some friend.

"I went out and called on three friends who were not at home. Then I went to the boulevards, determined to find someone I knew. It was dismal everywhere. A damp mugginess, that muggy weather which chills one suddenly, the depressing heat of fine rain dominated the streets, and seemed to tire and extinguish the gas lights. I walked along limply, repeating: 'I shall find nobody to talk to!' Several times I inspected the cafés, from the Madeleine to the Faubourg Poissonnière. Melancholy people, sitting at tables, did not seem to have even enough strength to finish their drinks.

"For a long time I wandered like this, and, about midnight, I turned towards home. I was very calm but very tired. My concierge, who goes to bed about eleven o'clock, opened the door for me at once, contrary to his usual habit. 'Hello,' I thought, 'some other tenant must have just gone up!'

"When I go out, I always turn my key twice in the lock. I found it simply shut, which struck me. I supposed that someone had brought up the letters during the evening. I entered. My fire was still burning and was even lighting up the room a little. I took a candle to light the sitting-room, when, looking in front of me, I noticed someone sitting in my arm-chair, with his back towards me, warming his feet. I was not afraid; of course not, not the slightest bit. A very reasonable supposition crossed my mind, that one of my friends had come to see me. As I had notified the concierge when I

went out, he had said I should be back, and had lent his
key. In a second all the circumstances of my return
came back to my mind! the immediate opening of the
street door, and my door merely closed.

"My friend, whose hair only was visible, had fallen
asleep in front of the fire while waiting for me, and I
went up to awaken him. I could see him perfectly, one
of his arms hanging to the right, his feet crossed, his
head a little to the left-hand side of the arm-chair — all
indicating sleep. I wondered who it could be. The
room was not very well lighted. I went up to touch his
shoulder! . . . I encountered the wood of the chair.
There was nobody there. The arm-chair was empty!

"Merciful heaven, how I started! I jumped back as
if a terrible danger had appeared in front of me. Then
I turned around once more. And I stood there, gasping
from fear, so distracted that I could not think, almost
fainting. But I am a man of calm temperament, and
soon my reason reasserted itself. I thought: 'I have
just had an hallucination, that's all!' And I reflected
immediately upon that phenomenon. At such moments
one thinks quickly.

"I had had an hallucination — that was an undeniable fact. Now, all the time my brain had remained
lucid, functioning regularly and logically. So there was
nothing wrong with my brain. Only my eyes had had a
vision, one of those visions which make naïve people
believe in miracles. That was just a nervous accident
to the visual organs; nothing more; perhaps some con-
gestion.

"I lit my candle. As I stepped towards the fire I
noticed I was trembling, and I suddenly straightened
myself, as if I had been touched on the back. Obviously
I was upset. I took a few steps. I talked aloud. I
sang some choruses sotto voce. Then I double-locked the

door of my room and felt somewhat reassured. At least nobody could come in. I sat down again and thought for a long time about my adventure. Then I went to bed and blew out the light.

"For some minutes all was well. I lay on my back rather peacefully. Then I felt I had to look about the room. I turned on one side. There were just two or three glowing cinders in my fire, enough to light up the foot of the arm-chair, and again I thought I saw the man sitting in it. With a rapid movement I struck a match. I was mistaken. I could see nothing. Nevertheless, I got out of the bed and hid my arm-chair behind it.

"Then I put out the light again and tried to go to sleep. I had not been unconscious more than five minutes when I saw in a dream, but as clearly as in reality, the entire evening's scene. I awoke in desperation and, having lighted up the room, I remained seated in bed, without daring even to try to sleep again. Yet, in spite of myself, sleep twice overpowered me for a few seconds. Twice I saw the same thing. I thought I had gone mad. When dawn came I felt cured, and I dozed peacefully until noon. All was over, really over. I had had fever, a nightmare, something. I had been ill, in a word. Yet I felt very foolish.

"That day I was very gay. I dined at a restaurant, went to a theatre, and set out for home. But as I approached the house a curious uneasiness came over me. I was afraid to see Him again. No, not afraid of Him, not afraid of His presence, in which I did not believe, but afraid of another disturbance of my vision, afraid of the hallucination, afraid of the terror that possessed me.

"For more than an hour I wandered up and down the pavement; then I felt too silly and entered. I was gasping so much I could not climb the stairs. I stood for another ten minutes on the landing outside my flat.

Then I had a sudden burst of courage, a stiffening of the will. I put my key in the lock, rushed in with a candle in my hand, kicked the door of my room, which was half-open, threw a frightened glance towards the fireplace, and saw nothing. — Ah! What a relief! What joy! What a deliverance! I walked about cheerfully, but I did not feel reassured. I kept turning around with a start. The shadows in the corners upset me. I did not sleep well, being awakened all the time by imaginary noises. But I did not see Him. No. That was over!

"Since that day I am afraid when alone at night. I feel that vision near me, around me. It has not appeared to me again. No, but what does that matter? since I do not believe in it and know that it is nothing. Yet it disturbs me because I never stop thinking about it. — One hand was hanging to the right, his head was bowed to the left, like a man who is asleep. . . . Stop! Enough! For heaven's sake. I don't want to think about it!

"Yet, what can this obsession be? Why does it last? His feet were quite close to the fire. It is madness; He haunts me; that is the truth. Who is He? I know He does not exist, that it is nothing. He exists only in my apprehension, in my fear, in my terror! Stop! That is enough! . . .

"Yes, it is in vain for me to reason about it, to resist. I can no longer stay at home alone, because He is there. I shall never see Him again, I know. He will never show Himself. That is over and done with. But He is there, all the same, in my thoughts. He remains invisble, but He is there. He is behind the doors, the clothes-press, under the bed, in all the dark corners, in the shadows. If I open the door or the press, I put the candle underneath the bed; if I light up the corners, the shadows, He is gone. But then, I feel Him behind me. I turn around, although I know that I shall not see Him, that I shall never see Him again. Yet, He is behind me again, none the less. It is stupid, but it is atrocious. What can I do? Nothing. . . . He is there because I am alone, solely and simply because I am alone!"

The man thus haunted can still keep his secret. He presents to the world, at this time, an appearance of health, happiness, and success. He is rich and popular, his works are read by every class, his exploits with women are the fable and the envy of Paris, and his bronzed face and powerful physique seem to be a guarantee of bodily strength corresponding to the healthy vigour of his writings. The occasional shadows, the stories of fear and madness and death, are no more than proofs of his intuitive genius, which can follow a clue down deep into the dark and secret places of the mind and heart. As yet none suspected that the tortures of the hallucinations increasingly described were drawn from his own sufferings, from the anguish of insomnia and headaches and jangled nerves. From these there is still temporary relief to be found in stimulants and anæsthetics, and for a while drugs provide a refuge from the Enemy. It was thus his friends saw him:

"A robust fellow, somewhat low-sized, but well built, with a broad forehead beneath brown hair, a straight nose, and a military moustache, a strong chin and a ruddy complexion. He had a strong, decided look, rather rough and without any of those finer shades which indicate one's social standing and qualities of mind. His hands, however, were fine and flexible, and he had attractive shadows about his eyes. . . . Very polite but never expansive. With a slight smile he allowed one to talk, and his smile was baffling. . . . However much he tried to dissimulate, his quiet indifference was obvious. Clearly he cared neither for

what one had said nor what he had replied, neither for
his interlocutor nor for himself. He had been on his
guard; that was sufficient. . . .

"How glacial this first contact was for the young
enthusiasts who had listened to Zola expounding in
lyrical formulæ audacious theories, or who had become
intoxicated by the caressing eloquence of Daudet, prodigal of vibrant images, picturesque traits, and luminous
summaries! Maupassant's conversation, whether in
private or in a crowd, usually consisted of the current
banalities and the stalest commonplaces. Was he so
convinced of the superfluousness of words that he reduced them all to a common futility, regarding an idea
nobly expressed as no better than a vulgar witticism?
It seemed so, when he received with the same detachment the chatter of the most authentic nobodies and the
remarks of the finest minds of the time. Not an ad-
mission or a confidence which could throw any light
upon his life or his work; parsimonious with what he
saw, he never told a characteristic story or uttered a
wise remark. . . .

"He seemed, moreover, to look upon art as a pastime,
literature as a useless occupation, at least; he reduced
love to a physical function, and suspected the motives
of the most meritorious actions. . . . Perhaps he over-
reached his object. As a result of hearing him deny
morals, art, and literature, of seeing him absorbed in
boating, of listening to him telling the story of his love-
affairs, which he did not always find in a very high class
of society, many people finally thought of him as one of
those terrible Normans who eat and fornicate their way
through his novels and stories with such superb ease and
such unconscionable amorality."

Flaubert's disciple, now that he was celebrated, in his
turn, showed no desire to emulate his Master's tireless

passion for literature and the problems of his craft. His little booklet on Zola, published by Quantin in 1883, was obviously an act of politeness, feebler in critical ideas than the study of Flaubert, and unredeemed by the enthusiasm and intimate knowledge which gave value to his account of his old friend. Contrary to what might have been expected from his early associations with the Flaubert circle and the Zola group, the now prominent writer avoided all literary society as much as possible. While the salons of Madame Aubernon and Madame de Caillavet waged bitter warfare over rising lions like Jules Lemaître and Anatole France, Maupassant was not counted amongst the possible candidates for such honours as these ladies procured for their favourites. He did appear occasionally in the drawingroom of the beautiful Madame de Loynes, who looked like the heroine of a play by the younger Dumas, whose discovery she was, but Madame Daudet recorded no pleasant memories of him, and the Grénier of Edmond de Goncourt saw him rarely. Princess Mathilde was more favoured, but when asked for her recollections of him she could only reply: "I knew M. Guy de Maupassant very well; I saw him often here. I liked him very much. . . . But I have nothing particular to tell you about him."

The list of his friends, almost all of whom are remembered in the dedications to the stories in *Contes de la Bécasse* and *Miss Harriet*, is significant. Apart from the Flaubert and Zola associations, they are writers of inferior fiction and journalists, the only important names being those of Bourget, Lavedan, Hervieu, and Porto-Riche. He was not identified with any of the literary movements of his day, save when he was, despite his convictions, linked with the Naturalistic school. His publishers were typical of his aloofness from all of the creative groups, being chiefly purveyors of boudoir fiction of a pseudo-erotic type.

Rouveyre and Bloud became insolvent after publishing *Contes de la Bécasse*, and Monnier's edition of *Clair de lune* was the only work on his list that is remembered except the startling early works of the bizarre young woman, Rachilde, whom Barrès saluted as "Mademoiselle Baudelaire." Havard never had any rival to Maupassant, who reigned supreme amidst now forgotten favourites such as Gustave Toudouze, René Maizeroy, and Jules Case, whose *Petite Zette* is dedicated to Maupassant. In return for this compliment Havard politely inquired whether Maupassant "could not do something for it just to oblige me." He avoided literary society, in short, even when selecting his publishers, for he might have been one of Lemerre's authors with Bourget, Daudet, Anatole France, and Paul Hervieu, or Charpentier's with Zola, Goncourt, Huysmans, and Céard. He preferred to be the one-eyed king in the kingdom of the blind, and had no relations with the publishers who were the rallying points for the various literary schools.

Maupassant could not unbend in bohemian society; even the gaieties of the Chat Noir were too much for him. His boating friends Edmond Deschaumes and Harry Alis took him to the famous cabaret on the Boulevard Rochechouart, where Rodolphe Salis, Maurice Rollinat, Edmond Haraucourt, Guy Charles Cros, and Alphonse Allais, amongst others, recited and sang for the amusement of themselves no less than that of a public which had not yet forgotten what a cabaret really was. Maupassant liked the long narrow room, lighted by stained-glass windows, and furnished in thirteenth-century style, and he was amused by the dark alcove which Salis had nicknamed the "Institute." At first nobody would sit in this gloomy place, except a young student who installed himself every day with an algebra, a book on geometry, a bottle of wine, and a flute. When he was tired of his equations, he drank a glass of wine and played his flute, delighting in the refuge which he had discovered. Once Salis had observed this ingenious device for being alone, he gave the corner its name, and it was greatly in demand — so much so that the student abandoned his studies and became one of the Chat Noir entertainers.

Maupassant relaxed for a moment, and allowed his name to appear as manager of the weekly review *Le Chat Noir*, to which Richepin, Rollinat, Samain, and others contributed, and where Maurice Donnay made his *début* with a sonnet, "printed on the last page, above an advertisement for suspenders, and with the author's name misspelt." The functions of the manager were wholly imaginary, but after a few weeks M. de Maupassant repented of his weakness and grew angry. He ordered Deschaumes to remove his name from the magazine, but the letter miscarried. Whereupon Maupassant asserted his dignity in a manner which is an interesting comment upon the state of his nerves and his curious frame of mind in this *annus mirabilis* of his: "I asked you by letter to remove my name from the cover of *Le Chat Noir*. I learn that a special number was distributed at the Press Ball and that my name still appears as manager. This joke, continued against my wishes, is in the worst taste and is so rude towards me that it must make me regret my relations with you, which have been completely devoid of any courtesy on your part. I warn you that this letter has been written and posted in the presence of witnesses, and that I have taken the necessary steps to have the last laugh in this matter." In further explanation of this tantrum Maupassant said: "For six weeks I have been receiving quite a number of abusive anonymous letters in which people went so far as to accuse me of having sold my name to *Le Chat Noir* for 40 francs! Of course, I paid no attention to these outrageous statements, but one of my friends who mixes a great deal in journalistic circles heard the same stupid remarks and reported them to me. People said that one evening I went to M. Salis and whispered: 'I need two louis. If you give them to me, I will authorize you to put my name on the cover of your paper.'"

Maupassant was clearly not himself when he decided to take so seriously a harmless joke, which assuredly did not bring his name into any more dubious company than that in which it had already appeared. Persecution mania, however, was soon to become another manifestation of his condition, and here, at the beginning of 1883, he was showing signs of that litigious hypersensitiveness which afterwards involved him in rash quarrels. Appearances are all in his favour, but behind that smiling, evasive exterior is a sorely troubled man. Hostesses who asked him to dinner found very frequently a silent guest on their right, who corresponded not at all to the stories that were current about him. Félicien Champsaur notes "an agreeable smile which expresses the profoundest indifference. . . . What does Maupassant think? He keeps his opinion to himself. His curious laugh is only skin deep. . . . It is good enough for the men. As for the women, they are his strength and his weakness. Would he rather be praised as a writer or as a male?"

There is one subject about which his flow of words increases out of all proportion to the paucity of his ideas. Once again he unburdens himself, and, having recoiled from the vulgar society of *Le Chat Noir*, he finds himself inspired by René Maizeroy's *Celles qui osent* to profound meditations:

"On the subject of sentimental love, which is merely the hypocrisy of copulation, you have developed theories which shock me by their very subtlety. . . . I can understand that this agreeable occupation should occupy a large place in the life of women; they have nothing else to do. In a man's life I am astonished that it can be anything but an easily varied pastime, like a good meal, or what are called sports. . . . I shall never be able to see why two women are not better than one, three than two, and ten better than three. It is natural to return to one more often than to the others, as it is natural to eat a dish often if one likes it. But to keep one always would seem as surprising and illogical to me as if a person who is fond of oysters ate nothing but oysters at every meal, all the year round. . . .

"We men adore women, and when we choose one temporarily, we pay homage to the entire sex. You can idolize brunettes because they are dark and blondes because they are fair; one because her piercing eyes touch your heart, another because her voice thrills your nerves; one for her red lips, another for her shapely figure. But, alas, as we cannot pluck all these flowers at once, nature has given us love, the sudden whim, the mad caprice, which makes us want them all in turn, thus increasing the value of each at the moment of passion. Now it seems to me that passion ought to be limited to the waiting period. Satisfied desire, having destroyed the charm of the unknown, takes from love its greatest value.

"Every woman conquered proves once more that they are all very much alike when in our arms. Idealists especially, who carelessly pursue the illusion of which they dream, must be crushed the day following each act of possession. We, who ask less of love, might have the right to be more grateful for the little it gives to men of intelligence and taste. . . .

"What husband would dare to take with his wife those delightful liberties with which lovers at once begin? And that, you will admit, is the greatest prize of love: the daring of our kisses. In love one must dare and dare again. We should have very few agreeable mistresses if we were not more enterprising than husbands in our caresses, if we were satisfied with the chill, monotonous, and vulgar habits of conjugal love.

"All women dream; they dream of the unknown, of what they suspect, of what they guess. After the first surprise of the first embrace, they begin to dream again. They have read and they read. At every moment phrases of obscure meaning, whispered jokes, unknown words overheard by chance, reveal the existence of things they do not know. Should a woman chance to ask her husband a question, he at once adopts an air of severity and replies: 'Such things are none of your business.' But she finds that such things are her business as much as they are any woman's. Besides, what are those things? So they do exist? Mysterious, shameful, pleasant things, no doubt, since people whisper about them excitedly. Prostitutes, it seems, hold their lovers by practices that are obscene and powerful. . . . Those things which one dares to do in adultery are very charming, perhaps. Once the thought, the desire, has entered a woman's head, her fall is near, very near.

"Finally she dares, but gently, slowly. She has certain reserves and limitations. This — yes; that — no. Once the first step is taken, these distinctions are astounding and funny, but common. One would imagine that, from the moment a woman had decided to experiment with love, with love that is forbidden, subtle, inventive, she would always ask for more, always want something new, always seek and always expect different and more thrilling kisses. But it is not so. Morality, strangely out of place, reasserts its rights. . . . They do not dare to do all the charming things which render life less sad.

"I wish a poet, a real poet, would sing them boldly one day, sing in daring and passionate verses the shameful things at which fools blush. It would require neither coarse words, nor obscenities, nor suggestiveness, but just a series of simple, frank little poems that were quite sincere. Do you remember certain poems which we often repeated, poems considered to be abominable, but which are as sweet as caresses? You have done something equivalent in prose. Let fools protest. Go on."

At the age of thirty-three he has the desires and the intellectual equipment of a college boy. Vague references to Schopenhauer and Herbert Spencer are frequent enough to suggest a philosophical basis for his general attitude towards life, but not to indicate a close acquaintance with their fundamental ideas. The profound pessimism and disillusionment which pervade all his stories, their repeated pictures of the dreary or the comic futility of human activity, are the expression, not of a reasoned philosophy, but of his instinctive reaction to the spectacle of life, a reaction largely determined by his own peculiar state of mind and body. "I am not a decadent brooding over my own soul," he declared; "I cannot look into myself, and the effort which I make to penetrate to the souls of others is involuntary, constant, and dominating. It is not an effort; I am, as it were, overwhelmed, absorbed by my surroundings. I surrender and am impregnated; I plunge into the influences about me."

Flaubert's procedure is not his; books are not the
nourishment with which he prepares himself to write.
He believes in description, not in analysis. "All the
seductive resources of language, its sharp outlines, its
unexpected evocations are weakened when it expresses
the transitions of sentiment rather than the appearances of sentiments. At bottom our art consists in
showing the secrets of the soul in such a way as to render
them visible, moving, and, above all, æsthetic. To my
mind psychology in fiction may be summed up as expressing the soul of man in terms of life." Yet, for all
this avoidance of analysis, despite his crude psychology
— or because of it? — the secret thoughts of his own
mind colour his work so deeply that his writings, which
seemed so often cynical and inconsequent, stand out in
retrospect as a consistent manifestation of the most
determined pessimism in modern French literature.

It is not the philosophical pessimism coming down
from Montaigne to Anatole France, the poetic despair
of Châteaubriand, the lofty resignation of Leconte de
Lisle, or the serene disbelief of Stendhal. It is a physical
disenchantment with life, which Maupassant sees as a
lugubrious or a ridiculous procession of human animals,
struggling with passions and appetites, against sickness
and death. Contrary to the present optimism of the
believers in heredity and progress, he offers his studies
to show how the well-born and refined can produce offspring who may become idiots, brutes, drunkards, parri-
cides, and prostitutes; that Nana and Jacques Copeau
are not necessarily the products of the tainted blood of
the Rougon-Macquart families.

Yet, it was at this moment that Jules Lemaître delighted readers of the *Revue Bleue* with a phrase about
Huysmans, shortly before sweeping them off their feet
with the famous essay on Ohnet: "Two stories about

prostitutes, the story of a man with diarrhœa, the story of a gentleman who hates sleeping alone, and another about a man who wants decent meat — such, in brief, are the romances of M. Huysmans." Wherefore the author of *Marthe*, *Les Sœurs Vatard*, *En ménage*, and *A vau-l'eau* was contrasted, as a pessimist, with the cheerful writer of such gay *fabliaux* as *Boule de Suif*, *Fou?*, *La Femme de Paul*, and *Saint Antoine*. If Huysmans had not so pointedly protested his indifference as to whether the duchess did, or did not, sleep with the marquis, he might have been classed with the bright story-tellers of the *Vie Parisienne* and *Gil Blas:* Gyp, Armand Silvestre, and Catulle Mendès, amongst whom Maupassant was classified by the sprightly professor.

To the general public his pessimism is as yet hardly noticeable, and he escapes adverse notice amidst the general preoccupation with the brutal candour of Zola, who had discovered that adultery was an evil which was preying upon the great middle-class of France, and had presented his curious case against that scourge in *Pot-Bouille*, thereby driving away vast numbers of his customers. *Au Bonheur des Dames* did not add to the gaieties of the season, during which most of Maupassant's friends had been active. Abel Hermant made his début, and Paul Bourget issued his first important book, the *Essais de Psychologie contemporaine*, which meant little to readers who were being supplied by Maupassant's co-entertainers with such things as *Le Roman d'une nuit* of Catulle Mendès and Gyp's *Autour du mariage*. Ludovic Halévy's *La Famille Cardinal* and Daudet's *L'Évangéliste* were saluted with a respect which was not generally extended to Léon Hennique's praiseworthy effort to live up to Naturalistic expectations with *L'Accident de Monsieur Hébert*, his only sustained piece of work since he and Maupassant had collaborated. Zola was satisfied, however, by this grotesque variation on *Madame Bovary*, this sardonic adultery, the "accident" that compels a husband to change his residence, but has no other consequences, pleasant or unpleasant, for any of the parties concerned. "It shows a remarkable feeling for human stupidity," said Zola. "The imbecility of your adultery is so true that it is horrible. The amorous conversations, especially, are astounding in their photographic cruelty."

Une Vie was assuredly the novel of the year according to all accepted contemporary standards, and if any rival seemed to be present it was Loti's *Mon Frère Yves*. His articles from Tonkin had been exploited to advertise the book, which appeared in the autumn, just as his descriptions of gouged eyes and yellow bodies riddled by repeated bayonet thrusts, of Annamites mowed down by ferocious marines, were causing a stir. Havard and Maupassant, who were by no means amateurs in the gentle art of publicity, must have envied the cunning of Lieutenant Viaud and the firm of Lévy. Loti, too, was a ladies' man of equal, but more romantic, reputation, and his literary career proceeded contemporaneously with Maupassant's, book for book, year by year, until the latter's death. Then it was demonstrated that one can love, if not wisely, then, at least, too well to be killed by the thing one loves. Had he been clairvoyant at this moment, Maupassant might with justice have cursed the irony of fate which bestowed upon this Huguenot all the gifts which he craved. Mouche and the Seine and La Grenouillère were poor, sordid substitutes for Aziyadé and the Bosphorus and Tahiti. For a man who loved the sea, neither the yacht, *Bel-Ami*, with its fatal Highnesses, nor the earlier *Feuille a l'enfers*, with its fateful *canotières*, could compare with a man-of-war on the oceans of the world.

That autumn, however, the gods were kinder than Maupassant's philosophy permitted. Loti was just another of those romantics whom Zola and his friends had dislodged from favour once and for all. Alexandre Dumas *fils* was reassuring. "You are the only author for whose work I wait impatiently." Life in Paris was, after all, agreeable for a fashionable author, and invitations were pouring in to the number of seventeen a day. Now that La Guillette was ready he could escape to Étretat, and having hired a valet, François, who refused to wear a livery, he departed with him for the country in November. But soon the weather became so bad, and the letters from Paris so numerous, that he left behind him the pleasures of feeding the goldfish and entertaining mysteriously muffled, handsome ladies, one of whom, François learned, was a friend of Napoleon the Third. "He gave her a title," the cook assured him. "She has a coronet engraved on all her jewels, and on every article in her house." But François was soon engaged in trying to get order into the flat in Paris. "There were books, pamphlets, newspapers, piled up against the walls, against the furniture, on the ground, anywhere. On the tables there were mountains of them. I cleaned and polished every day; it was labour lost. My master walked about from his washstand to his desk, with towels all dripping wet." They are still in the old flat in the rue Dulong, in the Batignolles quarter, from which Maupassant saw the railway embankment as described in the opening chapter of *Bel-Ami*.

Maupassant was dissatisfied with the unpretentious place, and with other things, notably with the results of a party which he attended at the house of an anonymous prince. François noted the next morning that he looked gloomy. "The evening before he had . . . brought home a red-haired young woman, not pretty, but rather pleasing. After breakfast she flew away, but not for long; she came back at four o'clock, had to wait till six, and at seven she was off again, as my master was dining out. The next day she was there again at nine in the morning. This lasted four days." Whereupon Maupassant left orders that she was to be put out, by force if necessary. The lady had assured him she was leaving for Vienna, and her failure to do so was becoming too embarrassing. He decided to move to the rue Montchanin, and to spend a couple of months with his mother and Hervé at Cannes. There he sailed and loafed and corrected proofs, and set fire to his bedroom, fortunately without the loss of any of his manuscripts. He gambled a little at Monte Carlo and seemed not very well disposed for work. Finally, he declared his intention of returning.

"I have had enough of this place! I cannot go two steps without having to take off my hat to all these Highnesses who swarm everywhere. They invite me too often to dinner. That tires me and does not always amuse me." Three volumes of short stories were due for publication in 1884, and his mind was full of a new novel. It was high time for him to return to Paris, where he arrived in March, suffering from the cold and feeling miserable. This susceptibility to the cold, strange in a hardy Norman, became more and more pronounced until his pursuit of the sun was the pathetic symbol of a quest for health and happiness which ever eluded him.

CHAPTER VII

SUCCESS

HILE collecting enough stories from the two preceding years to give Monnier the volume *Clair de lune* and Ollendorff *Les Sœurs Rondoli*, Maupassant worked right into March so that Havard also might have a book for the spring of 1884, *Miss Harriet*. He was very proud of this English name, contrasting its effectiveness with the *Miss Rovel* of Cherbuliez, which did not, he said, sound English at all. He also prepared the account of his journey to Algeria for publication as *Au Soleil*, and wrote his first study of Flaubert as a preface to the latter's correspondence with George Sand. In the meantime he had become involved in a literary correspondence of his own with a mysterious lady who was likewise impressed by English names, and who signed herself "Miss Hastings," that being the title under which *Miss Harriet* first appeared in the *Gaulois*.

"Obviously," she wrote in her first letter, "I should like to say exquisite and striking things to you, but it is very difficult to do that on the spur of the moment. . . . I regret it all the more because you are remarkable enough to make one dream romantically of becoming the confidant of your beautiful soul, that is, if it *is* beautiful. If your soul is not beautiful, and if you 'do not go in for that sort of thing,' I shall regret it, chiefly on your account, put you down as manufacturer of literature, and pass on. For a year now I have been on the point of writing to you but . . . several times I thought I was exaggerating about you and that it was not worth while. Then suddenly, two days ago, I read in the *Gaulois* that someone had honoured you with a charming letter and that you wanted the address in order to reply. . . . I became jealous at once, again your literary merits fascinated me, and here I am. . . . I shall always remain unknown . . . and I do not even want to see you. I might not like your appearance. I only know that you are young and unmarried, two essential points, even in the clouds. But I warn you that I am charming. This pleasant thought will encourage you to reply. I imagine, if I were a man, I should not like to have to do with a dowdy old Englishwoman, even by letter."

To the address R. G. D., Bureau de la Madeleine, Maupassant replied with great solemnity:

"My letter will certainly not do what you expect. I wish at the outset to thank you for your kindness and your compliments. Now let us talk rationally. You wish to be my confidant. By what right? I do not know you at all. Why should I tell you — an unknown person, whose mind, tastes, and so forth, may not agree with my intellectual temperament — what I might say verbally, in intimacy, to the women who are my friends? Would that not be an act of foolishness, of infidelity to one's friends? Does not all the charm of affection between men and women (I mean chaste affection) come especially from the pleasure of seeing each other, of talking face to face, and of catching again in thought, as one writes to one's friend, the lines of her face floating between one's eyes and the paper? How can one even write those intimate things, one's inner self, to a person whose physical appearance, the colour of whose hair, whose smile and look, one does not know? . . .

"To return to the subject of letters from unknown

persons. In the last two years I have received fifty or sixty. How shall I choose among these women the confidant of my soul, as you call it? If they are willing to show themselves and make acquaintance, as in simple and respectable society, relations of friendship and confidence can be established. If not, why neglect the charming friends one knows for a friend who may be charming, but is unknown? Or who may be disagreeable either to look at or to talk to? All this is not very gallant, I know, but were I to throw myself at your feet, could you believe me faithful in my moral affections? Pardon this reasoning of a man who is more practical than poetic. . . ."

With more wit and lightness of touch the answer came:

"Your letter does not surprise me. I should not expect what you apparently imagine. I did not ask you to be your confidant — that would be a little too silly. If you will reread my letter you will notice that you failed to observe the ironical and irreverent tone I employed. To answer me by confidences would be the act of a nincompoop, would it? Because you do not know me? Would it shock you if I were to tell you frankly that Queen Anne is dead?"

Maupassant is informed that his story *La Mère Sauvage* is an unoriginal and hackneyed piece of work, and then his correspondent proceeds to play with his seriousness:

"As to the charm that mystery may add, that all depends on one's tastes. It does not amuse you. Very good. But it amuses me hugely. I confess it in all sincerity, as I do my childish pleasure in your letter, such as it is. . . . If it does not amuse you, it is because none of your correspondents has succeeded in interesting you, that is all. And if I no more than the others

have been able to strike the right note, I am too sensible
to bear a grudge. Only sixty letters? I should have
thought you would be more pursued than that. Did
you answer them all? . . . My intellectual temperament cannot suit you. You must be very hard to please.
Indeed, it almost seems to me as if I knew you, such is
the effect of novelists upon silly women.

"Still, you may be right. Writing to you with the
greatest frankness (the result of the sentiment afore-
said), I may look like a sentimental schoolgirl, or even
an adventuress. That would be most annoying. Do
not apologize for your lack of poetry, gallantry, etc.
Clearly, my letter was very foolish. . . . Shall we, to
my regret, let the matter rest here? At least allow me
to express the wish to prove to you some day that I did
not deserve to be treated as No. 61. Your arguments
are sound, but based on false premises. I forgive them
as I forgive your erasures and your old woman and the
Prussians. . . . However, if all you need is a vague
description to draw to me the beauties of your insensi-
tive old soul, I might say: blonde, middle height, born
between 1812 and 1863. As for character . . . No. It
would look like boasting and you would see at once that
I come from Marseilles."

"I write to you because I am abominably bored,"
Maupassant answered, hastening to the defence of *La
Mère Sauvage*. "You reproach me with having used a
threadbare theme about the old woman and the Prussians. But everything is threadbare; I do nothing else;
I hear nothing else; all the phrases, all the discussions,
all the creeds are commonplace. . . . You know what
you are doing and to whom you are addressing yourself;
you have been told this and that about me, good or bad
— it matters little. . . . But think of my position.
You may, it is true, be a young and charming woman,

whose hands I shall one day be happy to kiss. But you
may also be an old concierge, fed on the novels of Eugène Sue. You may be a young literary lady, as hard
and dry as a board. By the way, are you thin? Not
too much so, I hope. I should be sorry to have a thin
correspondent. I completely mistrust the unknown.
I have been caught in absurd traps. A girls' boarding-
school corresponded with me through an assistant mistress. My replies were passed around in class. It was
an amusing trick, and I laughed when I heard about it
. . . from the mistress herself.

"Are you worldly, sentimental, or simply romantic?
Or, again, just a woman who is bored and who wants to
be amused? I am not, I assure you, the kind of man
you want. I have not an ounce of poetry in me. I take
everything with indifference, and I pass two-thirds of
my time in profound boredom. I employ the other
third in writing words which I sell as dear as possible,
regretting the necessity of plying this abominable trade,
which has brought me the honour of being distinguished
— morally — by you. Here are confidences. What do
you think of them? . . .

"What perfume do you use? Are you a *gourmande?*
What sort of ears have you? The colour of your eyes?
Fond of music? I do not ask if you are married. If you
are, you will say 'no.' If you are not, you will say
'yes.' "

A sketch of a stout man dozing on a seat under a
palm, at the seaside, beside a table on which is a glass
of beer and a cigar, accompanied the next letter: "Well,
for a weighty Naturalistic writer you are not stupid,
and my answer would take up volumes if my self-respect
did not restrain me. . . . We will first of all settle accounts about the commonplace, if you don't mind. It
will be rather a long task. . . . You are right, on the

whole.   But art consists precisely in making us accept
the commonplaces by charming us eternally, as Nature
does with her eternal sun, her old earth, and her men
built all on the same pattern and animated by pretty
much the same feelings.   But there are musicians who
have only a few notes, and painters who have only a few
colours. . . .

"And those other commonplaces of your painful profession!   You take me for a middle-class person who
thinks you are a poet, and you seek to enlighten me.
George Sand has already boasted of writing for money,
and the laborious Flaubert groaned over his excessive
toil. Well, that laboriousness is reflected in his work
Balzac never complained like that, and he was always
enthusiastic about what he was going to do. . . . To
sell dear is very good, for there never has been really
brilliant glory without gold, as the Jew, Baahrou, says
— a contemporary of Job (fragments preserved by the
learned Spitzbube of Berlin). — For the rest, everything
gains by a good setting. . . .

"So you are tired and take everything with indifference.   And you have not an ounce of poetry in you!
Well, if you think that will frighten me! . . . Now I
can see you. You must have a rather fat belly, a waist-
coat of dull material, that is too short, and has its last
button undone. Even then, you interest me. But I
do not understand how you can be bored. I myself am
sometimes sad, discouraged, or angry; but bored —
never! You are not the kind of man I want? I want
nobody. I think that men should merely be the acces-
sories of strong women. . . . And finally I will reply
to your questions quite sincerely, for I do not care to
play with the innocence of a man of genius who dozes
over his cigar after dinner.

"Thin? Oh, no; but I am not stout either. Worldly,

The private asylum at Passy
where Maupassant was confined
on January 7, 1892

sentimental, romantic? What do you mean? It seems to me there is room for all that in the same person. It depends on the moment, the opportunity, the circumstances. I am an opportunist, and particularly liable to moral contagion. Thus I may also happen to be lacking in poetry like you. My perfume? Virtue. *Vulgo:* none. A *gourmande?* Yes; or rather, hard to please. My ears are small, irregular, but pretty. Eyes, grey. Yes, fond of music, but not so good a pianist as that assistant in your girls' boarding-school. If I were not married, should I dare to read your abominable books? . . . What if I were a man? "

Maupassant pretended to believe this last suggestion, and after addressing his correspondent as a professor at the college of Louis-le-Grand, he wrote: "Let me begin by thanking you for the pleasant details as to your physique and tastes. I also thank you for the portrait that you have drawn of me. It is certainly a startling likeness! I notice some errors, however. (1) Less paunch; (2) I never smoke; (3) I drink neither beer nor wine nor spirits. Nothing but water. Then the beatitude before the 'bock' is not exactly my favourite posture. I usually squat on a divan in the oriental fashion.

"You ask me who is my painter. Among the moderns, Millet. My musicians? I hate music. In fact, I prefer a pretty woman to all the arts. I put a good dinner, a real dinner, the rare dinner, almost in the same class as a pretty woman. There is my confession of faith, my dear old professor! I think when one has a good passion, a capital passion, one should give it full scope, and sacrifice all others to it. That is what I do. I had two passions. I had to give one up. I have sacrificed gluttony, to a certain extent. I have become as sober as a camel. . . . I have a passion for violent ex-

"So I have deeply wounded you. Do not deny it! I am charmed and humbly beg your pardon. I asked myself: Who is she? She wrote me at first a sentimental letter, the letter of a dreamer, an enthusiast. It is a pose common amongst girls of a certain type. Is she one of that kind? Many unknown admirers are. So I replied in a sceptical tone. You were quicker than I, and your second last letter contained some curious things. I could no longer make out what sort of person you were. I kept saying to myself: Is she a masked woman who is amusing herself, or a practical joker? You know, the accepted way of recognizing ladies at the *Bal de l'Opéra* is to tickle them. The 'tarts' are used to it, and simply say 'stop!' The ladies get angry. I tickled you in a very improper way, I admit, and you are angry. Now I beg your pardon, and all the more so because a phrase in your letter has given me a great deal of pain. You say that my *infamous* reply (it is not 'infamous' that has touched me) has made you pass a bad day. . . . Pray believe that I am neither so brutal, nor so sceptical, nor so improper, as I have appeared to be. But, in spite of myself, I have a great distrust of all mystery, of the unknown and of unknown people. . . . I mask myself among people who are masked. . . . I have, however, succeeded in seeing a bit of your character by a stratagem. . . ."

This self-complacency was inevitably too much for the unknown young lady, as she at once admitted. " By writing to you again I am ruining myself for ever in your eyes. But that is all the same to me. I shall revenge myself, by telling you the effect produced by your ruse to discover my character. I was positively afraid to send to the post office, as I imagined the most fantastic things. *That kind of man* will close the correspondence by —— I spare your blushes. As I opened the envelope I was prepared for anything. I was moved, but pleasantly. . . .

"Because I am angry? That is not a conclusive proof, my dear sir. . . . How can I prove to you that I am neither a joker nor an enemy? And what is the use? It is impossible any longer to pretend that we were made to understand each other. You are not up to my level. I am sorry. . Nothing would have been more agreeable to me than to recognize in you all superiority — in you or in someone else. I want to talk to somebody. Your last article was interesting and, à propos of young girls, I even intended to ask you rather a daring question. But . . .

"A very delicate little piece of foolishness in your letter has set me dreaming. You are troubled at having hurt me. That is either silly or charming — the latter, I think. You may laugh at me. What do I care? There you had a little touch of Stendhalian romanticism. But don't be alarmed. You will not die of it this time."

At this point Maupassant made his final effort to attach his elusive correspondent to himself and to find out who she was: "Decidedly, Madame, you are not pleased, and you tell me, in order to show your annoyance, that I am very much inferior to you. If you knew me, you would know that I have no pretensions to moral or artistic worth. In fact, both amuse me. Everything in life looks alike to me, men, women, events. That is my true profession of faith, and I may add, though you will not believe me, that I rely no more upon myself than on others. Everything may be divided into boredom, farce, and misery.

"You say that you ruin yourself for ever in my eyes by writing again. Why so? You had the good sense to admit that you were hurt by my letter, to confess it in an irritated, simple, fresh, and charming way, that touched and moved me. I made my apologies by telling you my reasons. You have again replied very prettily, without disarming, showing a kindness still mixed with anger. What could be more natural? I know well that I shall now inspire you with utter mistrust. And the worst of it is that you will then not want us to meet. One learns more about another person by listening for five minutes than by writing for ten years. Why is it that you do not know any of the people whom I know? When I am in Paris I go into society every night. You might tell me to go on such a day to such a house. I would go. If you did not like me, you need not make yourself known.

"You need have no illusions about my person. I am neither handsome, nor elegant, nor unusual. That, however, should make no difference to you. Do you frequent Orléanist, Bonapartist, or Republican circles? I know all three. Will you make me take up my position in some church, museum, or street? In that event I should make conditions so as to be sure I did not wait for a woman who was not coming. What about an evening at the theatre, without your making yourself known, if you like? I could tell you the number of the box where I should be with friends. You need not tell me the number of yours. And the next day you could write: 'Good-bye.' Am I not more magnanimous than the French guards at Fontenoy? I kiss your hands, Madame."

His powers of persuasion and seduction did not avail, despite his legendary successes. The last letter evaded him as easily as the first:

"I understand your mistrust. It is not very probable that a respectable, young, and pretty woman would amuse herself by writing to you. Isn't that it? But . . . Oh, I was forgetting that all is over between us.

I think you are mistaken, and I can say so because I am going to lose all interest for you, if I ever had any. You will see how. I can put myself in your place. An unknown lady appears on the horizon. If the adventure is too easy, she will not attract me. If there is 'nothing doing,' she is useless and a bore. I have not the good fortune to be between the two, and I tell you that in a friendly spirit, since we have made peace. What I find very funny is simply to tell you the truth while you imagine that I am trying to mystify you.

"Although a red Republican, I do not go into Republican society. And I do not want to meet you. But do you not want a little element of imagination in the midst of your dirty Parisian adventures? An impalpable friendship? I do not refuse to see you, and I am even going to arrange this without letting you know. If you knew that someone was deliberately looking at you, you might look foolish. That must be avoided. Your terrestrial envelope does not interest me, but does mine you? Suppose you had the bad taste not to find me wonderful, do you think I should like it, however pure my intentions? Some day, perhaps — I even think I shall surprise you that day.

"Meanwhile if it tires you, let us correspond no more. I reserve the privilege, however, of writing to you when I have anything nasty to say. You are suspicious. It is very natural. Well, here is a concierge's way of finding out that I am not one. Now, don't laugh. Go to a fortune-teller, let her smell this letter, and she will tell you my age, the colour of my hair, my surroundings, etc. You can write to me her revelations. Boredom, farce, and misery. You are quite right. It is true even of me, but that is because I desire great things which I do not possess . . . yet. The explanation in your case must be the same.

"I am not so simple-minded as to ask what is your secret dream, although my illness has restored to me an innocence worthy of Chérie. What a naïve old man that Japanese Naturalist is, in his Louis XV wig!

"So you think that, having written, I could simply come and say: 'Here I am.' I assure you I should be deeply embarrassed. They say you like only big women with dark hair. Is that true? Why should we meet? Just let me show you my . . . literary charms. You have succeeded that way."

By October she was dead, this young woman who spoke so disrespectfully of Goncourt's *Chérie*, which had appeared in the spring, after the author had read the preface to Maupassant, George Moore, Huysmans, Zola, and Alexis, as his farewell to fiction. Lying on her sofa, dressed in white silk and fine lace, she and her dying friend, Bastien-Lepage, watched the summer pass, and knew that life was ebbing away from both of them. "I am thinner by half. For two months it has been possible to follow day by day the progress of this attenuation. It is no longer Venus Callipygous — it is Diana. In appearance I am well and live as usual. But I have fever every day. . . . Nightmare, hallucinations."

She still thought sceptically of Maupassant: "Disciples of Maupassant, do not attribute this condition to the sleeplessness of a full-grown girl." In June she read Daudet's new novel, *Sapho*, and merely shrugged her shoulders. "How Zola would execrate it! But he will not say so. If he disparage Daudet, whom should he praise? . . . He burns incense to Goncourt and Daudet so as not to seem to adore only himself."

Did she see *Yvette*, when it appeared in the *Figaro* during August and September? Maupassant was working on it at the time of their curious correspondence, and during the last weeks of her life he was discussing it in terms which throw a light on his strange conception of what was to be the last of his universally famous short stories. "I do not want to publish this novelette alone in a volume. It would look like attaching an importance to it which it does not deserve. As a piece of writing I tried, and I have succeeded in doing, a sort of *pastiche* in the graceful manner of Feuillet and Company. It is a romance, not a study; clever, but not powerful." The opinion of the only intelligent young girl who was ever associated with his life on the only attempt ever made by Maupassant to delineate such a type would have been illuminating. She alone had discovered his obsession and warned him of his monomania. But Maupassant's unknown was a most unusual young girl. The name she withheld from him was Marie Bashkirtseff.

Their letters had been exchanged amidst the pressure of circumstances that seemed more important to Maupassant than the friendship of a young woman for whom there was no place in the philosophy of *Celles qui osent*. He moved into his new flat and was much engrossed in the furnishings. The dining-room was to be dark red, the drawing-room Louis XVI blue, the bedroom yellow. Kakléter, the upholsterer, and two workmen toiled under Maupassant's orders, and amongst other things bookshelves were installed, to the great relief of François. By May the warm weather had come, and Maupassant was disinclined for work. He went by train to Maisons-Laffitte, then embarked in a yawl, and rowed down to Rouen. After four days he was back, having had a fine holiday, and François prepared for Étretat, where the summer and autumn were spent.

Maupassant's affection for Étretat appears in his writing at this time, as in such stories as *Le Modèle* and *Adieu,* and even his dread of cold weather could not

keep him away. "Étretat is always delightful, even in
February. I know of no place that is gayer, brighter,
more cheerful than this little countryside, down in its
little valley, by its crescent-shaped strand, terminated
by the two gateways, one a giant, the other a dwarf, but
both equally charming." He made efforts to improve
the unpretentious resort, demanding improved postal
and telegraph service, and striving to make Étretat a
fashionable watering-place comparable to Dieppe and
Trouville. He was the celebrity of the place, and the
influence of himself and his friends resulted in the construction of a huge hotel, with a theatre, a club, and
gaming-tables. The simple life of the Étretat described
in his stories from early memories was soon a thing of
the past. One of the very first events under the new
régime was the cremation on the seashore, at dead of
night, of an Indian prince, which Maupassant recorded
in *Le Bûcher*. "I have seen a man burned on a funeral
pyre and I feel I should like to disappear in the same
way. Thus everything is over at once. Man hastens
the slow process of nature. . . . The body is dead, the
spirit has flown. Purifying fire scatters in a few hours
what was once a living being."

His own life at La Guillette is divided between regular
work, from eight until eleven, on *Bel-Ami*, and entertaining his friends. He decides not to eat any breakfast,
on the ground that milk and coffee in the morning is a
meal "only fit for women." His eyes have to be bathed,
François notes, but otherwise he seems to be in good
health. Ladies came and went, of course, and Maupassant played bowls and croquet with them. "Often he
did not even give the ladies time to take their hats and
cloaks off in the house. Their wraps had to be spread
out on the small thorn-hedge separating the meadow
from the garden. The player threw himself into it with

such ardour that one might question if the author of *Une Vie* paid any attention to the intonation and the amiable speeches of the ladies, when they cried: 'Well played, my dear!' or 'Be careful, darling!' all of which the echo of the Fécamp coast repeated slowly, but accurately."

François vouches for the care expended on the spare room, and from him we learn that "a young American lady, who had published many novels in France, was the first to occupy the room on which he had lavished so much care. This lady was as intelligent as she was beautiful. One morning, as the girl who attended her was not there to give her breakfast," the astounded valet continues, "she said to me: 'François, you can very well come into my room and put the tray on the table. It does not disturb me, I am covered up in bed.'" To Maupassant she spoke contemptuously of the difficulties of writing, but she dwelt upon "the great difficulty which two people almost always have in understanding each other, when they love completely — you know what I mean — when they know how to give each other the greatest sexual pleasure. Once that happens, an abyss separates them." Maupassant did not smile, for this was a tragic topic. "He looked gloomy and I noticed his eyes contracting nervously."

The months passed uneventfully in hard work, for not only was *Bel-Ami* his longest book, but Havard was pressing him for a volume of short stories for the autumn, all of which had to be written between January and October. Before leaving Étretat in October Maupassant spoke to François about the novel. "I hope the book will satisfy those who are always asking me for something lengthy; there are pages and pages, and so closely written! There is one part for the ladies, which will interest them, I believe. As for the journalists,

they can make what they like of it." Then Havard
wrote to him that *Yvette* and five other stories would
not make a long enough book. "I advise you not to go
below 300 pages, and to give me four more stories of the
same length as the rest, which will give us 300 pages odd,
like the previous volumes. You can see that we have
lost no time on setting and proofs, just as you have lost
none on correcting the galleys. I will send you page
proofs and you can pass them for press. We might try
to bring out the book about the 25th of this month, if
that is agreeable to you. If you decide to give us more
manuscript, that will not delay the volume, for we can
hurry on with the setting while you are correcting the
page proofs." A week after this letter some of the additional material was appearing in serial form. For
some reason, no earlier stories were drawn upon for the
Yvette volume, so that it actually did not appear until
1885, when Flammarion also published two volumes,
Contes du jour et de la nuit and *Toine*, which included
stories dating back two years. The changes of publisher here are significant. Maupassant was driving
hard bargains, as Havard's correspondence shows:

"You bully me about your accounts with extraordinary harshness. You know to within a few hundred
francs what there is, and at our last meeting I told you
the money was at your disposal. . . . Our accounts
should, of course, be made up at the end of each quarter.
But if we had to make them all up in the first week following, it would be physically impossible. . . . As for
the volume *Des Vers*, I have not quoted the figures because I wanted to talk to you about this. So far, this
has not been a commercial success. Obviously my edition is hindered by the other. I have spent nearly five
thousand francs on manufacturing and two thousand on
advertising, and I am still far from getting my invest-

ment back. I think that you might be reasonable about this and help me a little to stand this strain."

Maupassant was not at all well. "My eyes are getting *worse and worse*. I think the reason is that they are greatly strained by work," he wrote in February. "I have finished *Bel-Ami*. I have only to reread and revise the last two chapters. Six days' work and it will be definitely completed." The large manuscript of 436 closely written pages, with few corrections, was delivered in March, and on the 5th of April the first instalment appeared in *Gil Blas*, where the novel ran until the end of May. Then Victor Hugo died, and lay in state beneath the Arc de Triomphe. The street lamps were dimmed with black muslin, and the flags bedecked with crêpe, while Notre-Dame was enveloped in mourning, as the procession marched to the Panthéon, without benefit of clergy, the illustrious corpse reposing, by special request of the deceased, on a pauper's hearse. A month Maupassant complained that the death of Hugo had been "a terrible blow " to *Bel-Ami*. They had sold only 13,000 copies in four weeks! "This is the book which prevented me from going to Étretat, for I am making great efforts to increase the sales, but without much success. . . . It is in its twenty-seventh edition. . . . As I told you we shall go to twenty or twenty-two thousand. This is gratifying, but nothing more."

The book had not prevented him from leaving Paris in April, when he went with friends on a tour in Italy and Sicily. He was suffering from some intestinal disorder, as he wrote to a neighbour at Étretat, and his eyes were "in very bad condition." Nevertheless, he wrote his impressions of Venice and Naples for *Gil Blas* and *Le Figaro*, and stored up memories for a later book of travel. Characteristically, his most original article was on the Venus of Syracuse, about which he expressed himself with a fervour transcending the purely æsthetic.

"She represents woman as she really is, the woman whom we love, desire, and wish to embrace. She is plump, with powerful hips and bosom, and rather heavy legs, a carnal Venus of whom one dreams as lying down on seeing her standing. Her drooping arm hides her breasts, and with the other hand she raises the piece of drapery with which she covers, by an adorable gesture, the secret place of the cult of Venus. The whole body is conceived and concentrated upon this movement, and all thought is centred upon it. This simple, natural gesture, so modest and so shameless, which hides and reveals, covers and uncovers, offers and withdraws, seems to define the entire attitude of woman on this earth.

"The marble is living. One would like to touch it, in the certainty that it will surrender to the touch like living flesh. The back is inexpressibly alive and beautiful. It shows, in all its charm, that undulating, soft line which runs from a woman's neck to her heels, and in which all the modulations of human grace are visible, in the outline of the shoulders, in the sweet softness of the sides, in the powerful and lovely slope of the hips, in the diminishing roundness of the thighs, and in the gentle curve of the calves growing slender down to the ankles. . . .

"She has no head! That makes no difference. The symbol is more complete. It is a woman's body, only a body, which expresses the real poetry of love."

Maupassant was also impressed at Naples by the offers of guides who endeavoured to lead the party into ways of complicated sin. "They had more suggestions than there were animals in Noah's Ark. The difficulties of victory inflame their imagination, and these Tartarins of vice, shrinking from no obstacle, would offer one the volcano itself if one showed the slightest desire for it." Maupassant's tastes were simpler, as Diego Angeli and Joseph Primoli noticed one night in Rome. Paul Bourget happened to be there at the same time, so the two Frenchmen were shown around the city by their Italian admirers, who took them to a low-class Maison Tellier in the Via Tor di Nona. "The girls exerted themselves in an endeavour to please the visitors. Maupassant succumbed to the ripe charms of one of the girls and left the drawing-room with her. When he returned later, he found Bourget sitting, looking very sheepish, in the same place and in the same position as he had left him. Whereupon Maupassant cried: 'Now, my dear man, I understand your psychology!'"

While in Palermo, his friends discovered that his story of a man who was afraid to sleep alone was more than a mere fantasia. Like the protagonist of *Lui?* who was marrying to escape from his own shadow, Maupassant employed the services of professional ladies, who duly reported that his intentions had been purely platonic. He wanted a companion to keep away the spectre of himself. He also displayed his peculiar sense of humour by asking a doctor, who had just examined a man killed in an accident, for a piece of human flesh, declaring that it made a pleasant dish, which tasted like veal. He had caused a stir in Paris a short while previously by pronouncing upon the excellence of female flesh for eating. "I took two helpings," he told his horrified friend Henri Amic. Less macabre, if still unusual, was the entertainment which he provided at a party, by putting out the lights and then displaying the electricity in his hair when he ran a comb through it.

His search for thrills took him to the room in his hotel, the Albergo delle Palme, where Wagner had been staying. "For a long time," the proprietor said, "he stood in front of the open wardrobe, still perfumed with essence of rose, which the composer used for his linen." He used a great deal of perfume himself and, like so many of his tastes, this one was also to inspire him with a morbid theme, when, in *Un cas de divorce*, the smell of flowers is studied as a supreme form of sexual gratification. Contrary to the wishes of his friends, he insisted on going down into the Capuchin Cemetery filled with mummified corpses, in order to experience all the horror of death, and to give himself the sinister illusion that he could never find his way out of that desolation, that "human charnel-house," that "carnival of death." The sepulchre of the living, however, caused him to shudder, as they passed the city asylum. He no longer could say "Lunatics attract me, because they live in a mysterious world of dreams, where everything they have seen and loved is made over again by them in such a way that nothing is ever impossible. . . . Only those who are mad are happy, because they have lost the sense of reality."

On returning to Rome in June Maupassant found all the newspapers with the reviews of *Bel-Ami*. *Le Gaulois* described it as "the novel of the hour. . . . Here we gaily swim in an ocean of mud. . . . My God, what people, what surroundings, what a world! . . . M. Guy de Maupassant is very talented but his *Bel-Ami* is very repulsive," and suggested once more that he might choose nobler themes. The *Revue Bleue* spoke of "a strong, striking book, but cruelly and repulsively true. . . . Irritating and exquisite, at the same time." Sarcey became quite plaintive in his reluctant admiration: "I hardly know of any work which is more attractive and morbid. While it stirs up the mud of perverse curiosity at the bottom of our souls, it disillusions one with human nature and takes all hope out of life. Why go on living in a world consisting only of low cads and infamous females? . . . M. Guy de Maupassant, with the indifference of a philosopher, spreads before us the loathsome mediocrity of the human race." Like all his colleagues of the press, as Maupassant had anticipated, Sarcey was particularly upset by what he regarded as a libel on the newspaper world of Paris.

George Moore's novel on a similar theme, *A Modern Lover*, had appeared in London two years earlier, and, by a curious coincidence, he was writing that summer in the *Figaro* a series of impressions of his own country, *Terre d'Irlande*, which later became known in English as *Parnell and his Island*. The accusations made against both authors were of somewhat similar character, but whereas Moore had to defend himself on moral grounds, Maupassant actually despatched a long reply to his critics from Rome, in which that aspect of the case is barely touched upon. His chief concern is to set himself right with the press:

"So the journalists . . . think that I have tried to describe the entire press of to-day, and to generalize as if all newspapers were summed up in *La Vie Française*, and their staffs in the three or four characters I have introduced. It seems to me that a little reflection would have shown them they were mistaken. I simply tried to relate the career of an adventurer like those with whom we daily rub shoulders in Paris, and who are to be met in all professions. Is he really a journalist? No. I take him at the moment where he is about to become a groom in a riding school. He was not, therefore, impelled by a vocation. I am careful to say that he knows nothing, that he is simply greedy for money and without conscience. In the first lines I show that he is a rascal in embryo, who will grow on whatever soil he falls.

The soil is a newspaper. Why this choice? it may be added.

"Why? Because in that world it was easier for me than in any other to indicate clearly the stages of my character, and also because journalism may lead anywhere, as is so often said. . . . The press is a sort of huge republic, extending on all sides, where something of everything may be found, and where one may do anything; where it is as easy to be an honest man as a scoundrel. . . . He has no talent. It is only through women that he advances. Does he even become a journalist? No. He passes through every department of the paper without stopping. . . . Having become a journalist by chance, through a chance meeting, . . . he uses the press as a thief uses a stepladder. Does that mean that honest people cannot use the same ladder?

" I come to another accusation. People seem to think that I wanted to criticize, or rather to indict, the press of Paris by inventing *La Vie Française*. If I had chosen a big paper, a real newspaper, as my framework, those who object would be absolutely right. But I was careful to take, on the contrary, one of those dubious sheets, . . . a sort of agency for a band of political and financial swindlers, which unfortunately exist. . . . As I wanted to analyse a cad, I developed him in the most appropriate surroundings, in order to bring out the character. . . . Have I revealed their existence to anyone? No. The public knows about them. Why, then, the complaints? Because vice triumphs in the end? Does that never happen? Could one not cite some powerful financier whose beginnings were as doubtful as those of Georges Duroy? . . .

"I have described shady journalism as one describes shady society. Is that forbidden? If people say that I see too much of the dark side of life, that I study only

*Front view of the Chalet de l'Isère where Maupassant
tried to commit suicide in 1892*

dubious characters, my reply is that one does not meet many virtuous and honest people in the circles described. I did not invent the proverb: 'Birds of a feather flock together.'"

This debate now seems a little irrelevant, but despite Maupassant's denial that he had any particular people in mind, two women who had been close to him in his early newspaper days were recognized, and the evident connection between the life he describes and that which he lived during his 'prentice years did not escape attention. There is as little imagination in *Bel-Ami* as in *Une Vie*, and as much actual observation and description from memory. As the latter summed up the life of the Normandy he knew, so the former was an epitome of the Paris in which he made his name. Allowing for the licence of the novelist, there is more of Maupassant in Georges Duroy than in the characters of the later novels who acted, at times, as his mouthpiece. As his encounter with Marie Bashkirtseff showed, and his efforts at a philosophy of sex, he had the gallantry of the *sous-off*, as Bel-Ami had the latter's physique, to which he owed his successes. Gaston de Lamarthe in *Notre Cœur* may describe the author in his last incarnation, as the great lover of fashionable ladies, but for the best years of his life Georges Duroy and he were brothers under their skins. Madame Lecomte du Nouy must have known it:

"The women whose slave he seemed to be did not stand so high in his thoughts as they imagined. He was not fooled. . . . He used to describe them to me, body and soul. And when I asked him: 'Can you love them after having analysed their petty feelings, their pose of philosophical erudition, the vulgarity of their souls, the lowness of their morals?' he used to reply: 'I do not love them, but they amuse me. I find it very amusing

to make them think that I am influenced by their charm.
What tricks they play to hold me! One of them has got
to the point of eating nothing before me but rose-pet-
als!'"   The hand is the hand of Maupassant, but the
voice is the voice of Bel-Ami. Georges Duroy might
have signed the prefaces of René Maizeroy and Paul
Ginisty.

The general public certainly was not deterred from
reading *Bel-Ami* by the truth or the untruth of its pictures of the Parisian press. When Maupassant told his
mother in July that its success had been hampered by
Hugo's death, the sales belied him. In September Havard wrote fairly cheerfully about "that ruffian *Bel-
Ami*, now in its thirty-seventh edition," showing that
ten more editions had been printed in the space of a
month or so. "The early part of the famous programme
I described to you succeeded perfectly — as you doubtless noticed. — The *Figaro* is the only one that did not
respond, but I expect to make a second assault in October with more success." Two offers for translation
rights came from Sweden, one a hundred francs, the
other two hundred. Maupassant decided in favour of
the latter, for again he was asking his publisher about
his accounts.

"We are working on your account," Havard wrote at
the beginning of October, "which will be sent to you in
two or three days. I can tell you now that you may
count on nine thousand francs or thereabouts. All my
accounts are settled quarterly, as you know, but the
first month after the quarter is taken up in making out
all the different accounts. When I can do it in advance,
you know by experience how willing I am to oblige you.
But this quarter, for instance, when more than two
thirds of the copies of *Bel-Ami* were sold to the railway
stations, I shall have to wait until the end of October

for the payment due to me, which will permit me to pay you.

"In short, on the 17th inst. I can send you 2000 francs, and 2000 on the 26th. You will have to wait for the balance until the end of the month. However, if you are in urgent need of more than what I have mentioned, you can draw on me by note payable at the end of October, as you have already done.

"I have received 200 francs from Mr. Suneson at Stockholm for the translation of *Bel-Ami*, with which you are credited. Singer and Wolfner of Budapest also want the right to translate *Bel-Ami* into Hungarian, to be sold in two volumes at a franc, bound in boards. . . . Shall I ask them also for 200 francs?" And with a final query as to second serial rights, he leaves the author until the end of November, when a hurried call is answered for a thousand francs, with a promise of more in a week. Either Victor Havard was a very unbusinesslike man of business, or Guy de Maupassant was living well up to his income.

He was buying antique furniture and curiosities for his flat in Paris and his villa at Étretat, for those which he had bought in Italy, according to François, had all been so badly packed that only two small statuettes survived the journey. He had guests for the shooting and was giving many parties both at La Guillette and in Paris. One of the most curious was a little dinner for four. Two very smart ladies arrived, both extremely stout and wafting the sweetest perfumes. Then the bell rang again and there entered a schoolboy, who seemed rather awkward and shy until they sat down to dinner. "At table he quickly regained his self-possession. He was charming, telling very funny stories of college rows, with the air of a youth who knows all about the inside life of those barracks for young men. He was

handsome, had a very delicate mouth, with a slight down
on his upper lip, an aquiline nose, sensitive wide nostrils,
large black eyes, and black curly hair. Plenty of champagne was drunk at dinner, and when the dessert came
on everyone was merry. Tiny feet were advanced
under the table and the scene became most comical.
The ladies made a regular assault upon the young man,
who held his own, and gave as good as he received.
Still with a touch of shyness, he did not hesitate to tell
them that he asked nothing better than to prove to
them that he was an obliging man and of considerable
prowess. The ladies roared with laughter, but the
schoolboy laughed less, and seemed to take his rôle seriously." Maupassant neither ate, drank, nor laughed,
but gnawed his moustache, and when he ordered coffee
François observed that his eyes were "red and moist."
At half-past nine the youth departed, and the ladies
begged in vain to know who he was. Next day François
learned that the boy was a young lady, a school-mis-
tress, whom Maupassant had recommended for a position. She repaid the obligation by playing this part for
the delectation of Maupassant and his friends.

In the autumn of 1885, still in search of health, Maupassant went to Châtel-Guyon in Auvergne. "I have
been making some wonderful excursions in Auvergne.
It is really a superb country, peculiarly unlike any other
place, and I shall try to convey an impression of it in a
novel which I am beginning." The novel was *Mont-
Oriol*, which was not published until eighteen months
later, when it became evident at once that the impas-
sive, cynical, and indifferent Maupassant was no more.
His sufferings were breaking down his reserve, but already the first signs of his second manner are visible in
Yvette. The first sketch of this story, *Yveline Samoris*,
which appeared in 1882, was just a typical brief, brutal

anecdote of a girl who commits suicide when she dis-
covers her mother's profession. After two years Maupassant is able to feel the subtleties of such a problem,
and to see more in it than a mere news item. He has
begun to allow sentiment to come into his calculations,
but he can still refrain from sentimentalizing, so that
Yvette's recovery, despite all temptations, is more true
and more poignant than the brusque logic of the earlier
version.

CHAPTER VIII

"THE MELANCHOLY BULL"

ITH the beginning of the New Year came the usual task of collecting a volume of the preceding year's stories, which gave Ollendorff *Monsieur Parent* for spring publication. Later work, chiefly of the first half of 1886, furnished *La Petite Roque* for Havard, and Maupassant could depart for the Mediterranean and write his novel. In March he is in Antibes, and his activities are reported to his friend Madame Lecomte du Nouy, the heroine of *Amitié Amoureuse*, that romance of their friendship which so horrified Madame Laure de Maupassant.

"I am sailing and working hard. I am doing a story of passion, very exalted, very lively, and very poetic. It is a change and it . . . is not easy. The sentimental chapters have many more corrections than the others. However, it is coming out all right; with patience one can adapt oneself to anything, but I often laugh at the sentimental ideas, very sentimental and very tender, which I achieve after an effort! I am afraid this will convert me to that kind of thing, not only in literature but in life. When the mind takes a certain bent, it keeps it, and sometimes it actually happens, when I am walking about the Cape of Antibes, a solitary promontory like the dunes of Brittany, that I begin to think such adventures are not so silly as one might believe."

He found, however, that he could make little progress unless he refreshed his memories of Auvergne; so, after

death, and the famous story that gave its name to the volume published in 1887, after *Mont-Oriol*. The one may still be regarded as a piece of fiction — a not very effective "thriller" — heightened by effects that were suggested by authentic experiences. The other, *Le Horla* as it is universally known, is a clinical document, a case history, which any psychiatrist might have written down.

This diary of a neurasthenic might be paralleled at every entry by similar passages in Maupassant's correspondence and his travel books. He first complains of attacks of sudden and groundless melancholy; the fear of something invisible, of an approaching danger, which increases as the shadows of night grow deeper. He has atrocious nightmares. When alone in the woods, mad terrors pursue him. He clearly sees the disintegration of his reason, and this constant, lucid analysis of his mental state aids the progress of his malady. He argues in vain with himself, quoting recent discoveries concerning magnetism, hypnotism, and somnambulism. As he studies his own hallucinations, imminent insanity adds to his horror. His mind is still clear. But his courage and his will power weaken. "I am lost! Someone possesses my soul and governs me! Someone directs all my actions, all my movements, all my thoughts! . . ." He feels that there is someone behind him; an invisible hand seizes a flower before his eyes and crushes it, turns the pages of the book he has left on the table. When he looks in the mirror he is invisible until the phantom makes way for him. All the springs of his physical being are broken; his energy is gone; his muscles are relaxed; and flesh and bones are dissolved into water. The house is haunted; the invisible Presence is always there; no locks can keep him out. In brief moments of respite the awful future before him

terrifies him. One night he feels that the intruder is
present. He will burn this house down and the Horla
with it. Everything is consumed in the flames, but the
Horla lives; he will return. He cannot be killed. "Then
. . . then . . . I shall have to kill myself."

Maupassant himself is the patient whose "pulse is
rapid, eyes are dilated, and nerves upset," and who is
ordered to take cold douches and bromide of potassium.
Passionately fond of life, he, too, asks "whence come
those mysterious influences which change our happiness
into discouragement and our confidence into distress."
From the story to his letters is but a step: "I have not
a taste which I cannot renounce, not a desire which
isn't indifferent, not a hope which does not make me
laugh or smile. I wonder why I exert myself, why I
travel here and there, why I give myself the odious task
of earning money that I get no pleasure in spending.
. . . I am incapable of really loving my art. I criticize
and analyse it too much. I am too conscious of the
purely relative value of ideas, of words, of the most
powerful intelligence. I cannot help despising the mind,
it is so weak; form, because it is so imperfect. In an
acute and incurable form I have a feeling of human impotence, of our efforts which end in miserable make-
shifts."

Yet, by dint of following the sun, he can recover his
illusions for the moment. "I am in sap, it is true. Finding here the first awakening of spring, my whole plant-
like nature is stirred, causing me to produce these
literary fruits, which blossom from me in some way
which I do not understand." In spite of mental and
bodily ills, *Mont-Oriol* was finished at Antibes, in that
sunlit, five-windowed study of his, looking out on the
pine-covered hills, dotted with pink and white cottages,
on the chain of the Alps stretching out to the frontier:

Nice, the Promenade des Anglais, the Golfe des Anges, to the north the Golfe Juan and the Islands of Lérins. In December the faithful Havard wrote an epistle which sounded a note to which Anglo-Saxon ears are unaccustomed in gentlemen of his occupation, and also the first perspicacious comment upon this transition work.

"This time I made an obstinate and unheard-of effort not to touch *Mont-Oriol* until it was all printed. I wanted to get a single impression, unspoiled by interrupted reading, so I read it the other night at one sitting and without a break, and I am dazzled, overwhelmed; it moved and disturbed me so much. I am still quite upset. Never has any author, whether one of the immortal classics or amongst the living, touched me as you have — not even Victor Hugo, who, in spite of sublime flights, does not convey a feeling of real life like you. . . .

"I may as well confess, my dear illustrious apparent sceptic, that I wept at the end of the volume, and so did everybody with me. And in spite of your perpetual irony and jokes, we wretched middle-class philistines are not ashamed of it. In short, without waiting for the judgment of posterity, I declare that this is a sublime and imperishable masterpiece. It is Maupassant to the fullest extent, and in the plenitude of his genius and the complete maturity of his marvellous talent. Here you strike, with unusual power, a new note which I have long felt was in you. I had a forewarning of this accent of tenderness and supreme emotion in *Au Printemps, Miss Harriet, Yvette,* and elsewhere.

"I find this masterly work admirably orchestrated, with extraordinary moderation and sureness of touch. How the stages of poor Christiane's passion are graduated, and how dignified her sorrow! — And old Clovis, an immortal type, etched in bronze!

"Yesterday morning I talked about it to Wolff so enthusiastically that he wanted me to send it to him at once, so that he could write an article about you. And without asking your permission, I have done so. But I wish now that the announcement in *Gil Blas* had been delayed a few days.

"Finally, this book should bring us from twenty to twenty-five thousand new readers, for it will suit the most timid bourgeois souls, whom you persistently frightened by your earlier productions."

While Maupassant was recovering from the surprise of this bouquet and deciding that it was about time for him to double his charges to translators, Edmond de Goncourt also had a moment of agreeable astonishment. The niece of the United States *Chargé d'affaires* — "a very charming person " — made him an offer of eighteen hundred francs for the play, *Renée Mauperin*, nearly three times as much as Maupassant received for his infinitely more popular works. But what most impressed Goncourt and Céard, his witness, was that the money was paid immediately in cash, and "by a new process the contract was immediately printed on a kind of piano."

The date was December, 1886, and *Mont-Oriol* began to appear in *Gil Blas*, running as a serial until February, when it was published in book form. The critics were all smiles, and spoke evidently in anticipation of those additional members of the bourgeoisie who had been deterred by the pessimism and the improprieties to which the reviewers now ceased to allude. Maupassant is received into the fold, and from this point onwards his works are discussed in a more sympathetic and respectful manner than that reserved for the nasty Naturalists.

Brunetière at once sets the tone: "I should regard it as a serious oversight if I did not add that in *Mont-Oriol*

M. de Maupassant's customary harshness is considerably modified; he is still a pessimist, it is true, but there is a smile in his pessimism. Emotion has heretofore been lacking in his novels, and we are happy to find it in *Mont-Oriol*." André Hallays was more specific, in the *Journal des Débats:* "Ever since *Boule de Suif* appeared in *Les Soirées de Médan*, what has not been written about the robust talent of the author, his clear, vigorous style, the sober power of his descriptions, the bitterness of his humour, the tragic quality of his comedies? All these qualities — and others — are present in *Mont-Oriol*. His observation is less brutal without losing its precision and vigour, the style less strained, the narrative more lively. Here and there the remarks are almost feminine; there is charm, *abandon*, even prettiness. The fundamental irony of the story is veiled in a gentle melancholy. . . . And, what is more remarkable, beyond the plane on which the characters move there suddenly appear distant and unexpected flashes of general ideas." After reading his advance copy, Albert Wolff said: "This tender note, devoid of rhetoric, coming after so many pages that sparkle with observation, ends the volume with a note of feeling that will endure."

Contrary to Havard's predictions, the sales of *Mont-Oriol* had been unsatisfactory during the early months of 1887. Those faithful customers, the railway bookstalls, had taken only 3200 copies, and a puff which Havard had arranged for did not appear in *Le Gaulois*, having been rejected by the owner of the paper after it was in type. Rumours of war with Germany were credited with a general slump in the bookselling business. Maupassant told his friend at Passy that Zola's pacifist leanings during the crisis were absurd, and his patriotic utterances, as he rowed her on the Seine in the

June twilight, were duly entered in the diary made with his own hands.

On his return from the South of France he had soon tired of Paris. "He sees too many people and, above all, receives too many invitations. They will not leave him alone," says François, adding a typical incident by way of comment upon that last sentence. "He was out one afternoon when a small yellow dog-cart stopped before the house. A young lady dressed in a pretty tailor-made grey costume, with a hat to match, jumped down. I opened the door, and she asked me sharply if M. de Maupassant was at home." On hearing that he was not, she went in and, taking a sheet of paper in his desk, "wrote one word in large letters filling the page: 'PIG!'"

When he returned Maupassant saw the omen and acted as he always did when his romances became — as they always did — wearisome. "The young marquise," he explained, "who writes so well is the daughter of a former minister of the Second Empire. But I will not see her — I am completely tired of her. . . . I will not stay here in Paris; they will not leave me a moment to myself. It is terrible! . . . I have just rented a place at Chatou."

"The devil take all these women!" he cried as they set out for Chatou, where he had taken a flat for six weeks, between the two arms of the Seine, near the bridge. In a sort of turret looking out on the river, he fitted up his study and, although his eyes were so sensitive that the little room had to be darkened, he prepared to work. Even with one window blocked up and the blind of the other pulled down, the light was too strong, so he retreated to the drawing-room. The view of the muddy banks of the Seine at low tide depressed him, but the innumerable frogs suggested one of his strange prac-

tical jokes.   A basketful was collected and François was
despatched to a lady friend, with strict orders not to say
what was in the basket.   But he gave the secret away,
explaining that *cuisses à la poulette* made an appetizing
dish.   Whereupon the lady thought she saw a light.
"Oh! Is that it? . . . yes, the *thighs* are the interesting part!"   And François was dismissed in a burst of
laughter while the frogs were transported to the Bois de
Boulogne.

"I hope I shall be less persecuted by people," Maupassant had said, but at once the parties began again,
with the usual preponderance of one sex.   "We shall
be twelve at table . . . and there will be only three
men . . . What is most amusing is that they are
nearly all countesses. . . . Excepting Madame — and
little Nina — each of them bears the coronet of a count-
ess."   The entertainment provided was a friend of Maupassant's who told the ladies where their husbands were
and how much they enjoyed their favourite haunts.
The listening François gathered that the gentleman had
often accompanied the absent husbands to the houses
which he described so graphically.   "The conversation
might seem rather rough, but the noble ladies were not
upset by such trifles, for they all proclaimed their indifference to the details he had just given them, with which
they had long been familiar.   They said that their
husbands preferred tainted restaurant meat to good
fresh beef in their own homes.

"Don't be anxious on that account," they concluded,
"you handsome creature with dark brown hair.   We
have not waited for your revelations before making
good use of the liberal gifts of heaven, and having as
much fun as we could manage to get.   We leave our
spouses to their own tastes, of which the least said the
better."

Other visitors were of a more dramatic turn: One lady arrived for the purpose of seeing Maupassant and shooting him. He was warned, so she contented herself with swooning, until he finally came back to the house and soothed her, "as calm as if this was quite an every day occurrence," said the valet to whom he was a hero.

The house was full of people who came on boating parties. Maupassant kept a large crowd all night by causing them to miss the last train. Much champagne was drunk and the guests drew lots for the limited sleeping accommodation. But these days on the river did not always end so hilariously. "I am very fit," Maupassant said one day to François, showing him his arms. "There is strength here. . . . And with this chest of mine I can both breathe freely and bear up against fatigue, which is not the case with all these amateur rowers. I am ready to show them what I can do, if they will stand up against me."

Off he went in "white jersey and knickerbockers, and a magnificent white yachting cap," boasting of his fine condition. "It was more than six when he came in; his face was distorted and pale, with violet patches; the sight terrified me.

"'Quick, François,' said he, 'my shower-bath immediately.'

"I helped him to take off his jersey and breeches; his body had a livid hue. Nevertheless, he took his shower-bath, and I began to rub him with a horse-hair glove and eau-de-Cologne. . . . He continued the rubbing for a long time, but he could not obtain the usual reaction. Then he wanted to tell me about the boating-party, but his voice failed him. He chopped his words and could not pronounce them."

After this warning Maupassant was morose for several days. "I do not feel well; I always have a pain inside.' The pains got worse, and "all the remedies usually employed in similar cases failed to relieve him. He then resolved to take every quarter of an hour fifteen drops of perchloride of iron in a little water, continuing to apply linseed poultices with laudanum, and that stopped the pain." He went to Paris, but his doctor could not help him. He came back dissatisfied, and his irritation was such that he denounced an American admirer for an innocent offence. "A rich American has offered me a steam yacht! What could the millionaire think of me, when he made this proposal? Was he dreaming or was he *drunk?* "

Then he became immersed in the romantic ecstasies which his lady in Passy provoked. Again he rowed her in the twilight, and he enchanted her ear with a discourse about the Seine, varying in its moods like a woman, holding for him the same fatal fascination. "To-day everything seems perfect: the air I breathe, the landscape about me, and your adorable presence. Even the fugitive thoughts passing through my mind are happy. I am young and healthy; I am loved and in love; I am a Frenchman, and my country esteems me. What more do I want? "

What he wanted was health of mind and body. He felt again the urge to move away in search of it. "It is too damp for me here. This place between the two arms of the Seine is never dry." They went down to Étretat, and, most appropriately, he wrote the final version of *Le Horla*. On the principle of grasping a nettle, he told François, when the manuscript was completed, that when the critics read it they would say he was mad. But it was not until a few years later, when the facts were undeniable, that this document came to be regarded as pathological. At first it merely seemed to be a rather surprising essay in the manner of Poe, like other stories of madness which preceded it; the recent *Petite Roque*, for example. He had written very few stories since the beginning of the year, and in order to make up a volume for his publisher he drew on material dating back several years. He had passed the period of amazing fecundity, and from now on the flow of stories diminishes. Havard had to content himself with reissuing *Contes de la Bécasse*, of which he had few hopes because of its "old-fashioned, eighteenth-century title." *Ce cochon de Morin* would be tremendously effective, but he was afraid to call the work by a title which would be "too loud."

Madame Lecomte du Nouy came over from her villa close by and heard the theme of *Pierre et Jean*, and they went to Le Hâvre together to get local colour. He was suffering greatly from insomnia, and his eyes were so weak that she read a great deal to him, chiefly from the letters and memoirs of ladies who had also enjoyed the charms of *amitié amoureuse* a century earlier — Mlle. de Lespinasse, Madame du Deffand, and the Marquise du Châtelet. The atmosphere of the period so affected Maupassant that he presented his friend with a poem, which was later used in evidence against the platonic theory of their friendship:

> Mars trouva Vénus à Paphos,
> La belle dormait sur le dos,
> Voyons, dit-il, tout ce qu'elle a,
> Alleluia !

> Il alla déranger soudain
> L'écharpe qui couvrait son sein;
> Plus blanc que neige il le trouva,
> Alleluia !

Sa main eut la témérité
D'en tâter la rotondité,
Le sentant ferme il s'écria
    Alleluia !

Enivré de si doux plaisirs
Il forma de nouveaux désirs,
Et de baisers se regala,
    Alleluia !

De cent façons pour l'admirer
Il se mit à la revirer . . .
Ce qui s'augmente s'augmenta,
    Alleluia !

Vénus fermant toujours les yeux,
Se plaça pourtant de son mieux,
Et le guerrier en profita. . . .
    Alleluia !

A peine un jeu se finissait
Qu'un autre se recommençait;
Trois jours entiers cela dura,
    Alleluia !

Mais enfin Vénus s'éveillant
Dit au dieu presqu'en rougissant
Et quoi, Monsieur, vous étiez là ?
    Alleluia !

Walking in his avenue of ash trees he composed *Pierre et Jean* and, with the copious assistance of ether, what is considered his purest and simplest novel was completed in September. The story, he told Hélène Lecomte du Nouy, had been suggested to him by the fact that a friend of his had inherited a fortune from an old

friend of his family. As the father was an old man and
the mother young and pretty, Maupassant set out to
explain how such a fortune was left to the son.

He had been out of touch with his friends in Paris,
having had a tiff with Edmond de Goncourt over the
latter's alleged refusal to contribute the balance of the
money required for the Flaubert monument. Goncourt
had resigned from the committee, but, after a personal
appeal and an apology from Maupassant, he recon-
sidered his decision, without, however, revising his opinion of him. Maupassant was, therefore, as surprised as
most people when he discovered in the *Figaro*, one
morning in August, that a third group of Five had burst
in upon the scene. His own Five had been the disciples
of Zola, the new Five constituted a deliberate anti-Zola
offensive. *La Terre* had been appearing as a serial, and
these young men declared that the time had come to
protest against such filth. They indulged in a vast
amount of irrelevant words, of dreadful scientific jargon,
and paid special attention to the physical and psychological deficiencies of Zola, kidney disease, impotence,
and caprology.

"In the name of our sane and virile ambitions, or our
cult, our profound love, our supreme respect for art,"
they protested. And their names were Paul Bonnetain,
J. H. Rosny, Lucien Descaves, Paul Margueritte, and
Gustave Guiches. Zola had defended Bonnetain, when
the latter surpassed him in *Charlot s'amuse;* Margueritte's first novel, *Tous Quatre*, had portrayed Lesbian
love and scenes worthy of Petronius; Descaves was
one of the authors of Kistemaeckers, not renowned exactly for the virtuousness of his publications. Only
J. H. Rosny and Gustave Guiches were within their
rights in casting, if not the first stone, at least the stone
which was to mark the last resting-place of the Natural-

ist movement. Anatole France, in an article violently denouncing "the Georgics of filth," rejoiced that the author of *La Terre* had suffered the fate of Noah. "Five of his spiritual children have committed the sin of Ham. . . . They have publicly mocked at their father's nakedness."

Zola, as usual, showed that quiet common sense of his, which always placed him, even when in the wrong, at an advantage over his enemies. None of the writers, except Bonnetain, was even known to him, and he wondered why they repudiated him. "If friends of mine, if Maupassant, Huysmans, and Céard, had addressed me in such language publicly, I should certainly have felt somewhat offended,' but he expressed his satisfaction at the thought that his disciples, so called, had betaken themselves off, for he had always declared that he had none. Huysmans, Céard, and Alexis expressed their sympathy with him, but Maupassant remained silent. His position was ambiguous, because he had been saying privately for some time past what the five newcomers had openly confessed, but Zola apparently never knew exactly what Maupassant thought of him, just as he seemed to be unconscious of Edmond de Goncourt's repressed but visible hostility.

Soon, however, Maupassant himself was the subject of some excitement at the offices of the *Figaro*. He had written a preface to *Pierre et Jean* which the literary supplement of that journal had agreed to publish, and the novel itself was serialized in the *Nouvelle Revue*, during the months of December and January. Early in the latter month, the preface was published with certain omissions about which the author had not been consulted. He was excessively irritated, and at once brought an action for damages against the paper, in addition to addressing this peculiar communication to the editor of the *Figaro*, who was not responsible for the literary supplement:

"Yesterday the literary supplement of the *Figaro* published an essay of mine on the Contemporary Novel, in which I cause Flaubert to look foolish by attributing a phrase of Buffon's to Châteaubriand. I wish to say that the silly mistake was mine. I do not know how I could have been so careless, having heard the quotation so often from Flaubert's own lips.

"If I address myself to you in order to make this correction, and not to the place where my essay appeared, it is not because of the inconsiderate and inexplicable conduct of the *Figaro* towards me, but because I wish to proclaim once again the absolute right of every writer to defend his ideas, whatever they may be worth, against all possible *tampering*.

"Three months in advance I was assured that the *Figaro* had accepted my essay, to which, whether rightly or wrongly, I attached considerable importance, because it explains my views about fiction, and is an answer to the criticism so often brought against me. Had it been refused, I should have had time to choose whatever review I liked.

"I delivered the manuscript three weeks before publication. The Editor of the supplement made me delay for a week the publication of *Pierre et Jean*, to which the dissertation serves as a preface, in order to leave the issue of January 1 to the review of Caran d'Ache. . . . I have, therefore, not only the right, but all the circumstances are in my favour and, consequently, it is my duty to obtain a decisive judgment against the irresponsible blue pencil, however competent the hand that wields it."

Maupassant's lawyers were evidently embarrássed by their excited client's demand for five thousand francs

damages, and by his claims to literary grandeur expressed in terms which were a denial of the fact. After
various negotiations, and with the conciliatory co-oper-
ation of Ollendorff, who published the book shortly
afterwards, the Editor of the supplement agreed to
print an explanation and apology, which satisfied Maupassant. Each party paid his own costs, and the first
public symptoms of the author's paranoia were forgotten.

The preface in question was neither better nor worse
than most of Maupassant's attempts to theorize about
literature, and contains the gist of all his previous utterances on the subject of the novel. The inevitable in-
vocation of Bouilhet and Flaubert is heard; there is a
dig at the artificial style of Goncourt, which Edmond
did not forget; an oblique shot at Bourget's psychological novels; and the plea, so often made, for the development of characters through action. Were it not for
the description of Maupassant's training under Flaubert, the preface would long since have been forgotten.
It was a very ponderous document to precede so short a
novel, and one suspects that, had *Pierre et Jean* been
longer, the volume would not have been padded out by
such a dissertation.

The critics were kind, if sometimes facetious about the
preface. Having heard a word in defence of the criticism of fiction, readers of *Le Temps* were assured that
Maupassant had "treated an ungrateful subject with
the sure touch of a talent in full possession of itself.
Suppleness and proportion — nothing is lacking in this
robust and masterly story-teller. He is powerful without straining; his art is consummate." Thus spake
Anatole France, or rather Madame Arman de Caillavet,
who so often wrote his articles for him. "I have been
amusing myself lately writing a little preface for

Adolphe. . . . It will appear under the signature of
Anatole, from whom it was ordered. . . . Now I am
putting a few ideas down on paper for the next article
in the *Temps,* on Maupassant's novel."

Maupassant's own view of *Pierre et Jean* is expressed
in a letter to his mother, shortly before the first instalment appeared: "It will be a literary but not a commercial success. I am certain it is a good book, as I have
always told you, but it is cruel, and that will prevent it
from selling. I shall, therefore, have to find a way of
earning my living without depending too much on my
publishers. I shall try the theatre, which I regard as a
business, in order that I may be able to write my books
exactly as I like, without caring in the least what happens to them. If I can succeed in the theatre I shall
sleep peacefully, but without indulging too much in that
pseudo-literary traffic. . . . Only the theatres are full
and making money, for people must spend the evening
somewhere. I am going myself just now in order to
learn how things are done, and I see that everything has
to be learnt all over again from the beginning."

The note of anxiety about money and the desire to
write profitable plays now become frequent. Yet, at
the end of the first quarter of 1888, Havard is writing
that his royalties for those three months are two thousand francs, despite the political unrest, and a very bad
season for booksellers. Maupassant is ill and relatively
unproductive. When he tries to make up a collection of
stories to accompany *Le Rosier de Madame Husson* he
has to go back to things published in 1883 and 1884.
The years when sixty, forty, or even twenty stories were
there to be selected from are gone. In 1887 he wrote
only ten, in 1888 only five stories. The hour-glass is
visibly running out. While Pierre Loti's rouge and high
heels and unattractive presence are obstacles which he

soon overcomes on the road to romance with the Queen of Roumania, Maupassant is trying to compensate himself with social adventures which in rational interludes he despises, but which are making him the laughing-stock of Paris. He flees again to Africa, to his yacht, his "floating solitude." He is incessantly on the move. Algeria and Tunisia, but first Aix-les-Bains. There Taine meets again the man he remembered as a youth at Flaubert's. It is a very different Maupassant, and Taine finds the epithet which describes him: *le taureau triste.* "The melancholy bull " now realizes that something is radically wrong, but he does not yet know the worst.

A clear picture of him at this stage is furnished in *Sur l'eau,* an intimate diary, "relating no story, no interesting adventure," but telling more about him, in his own words, than all his works put together. Cruising in *Bel-Ami* he is far from all distractions; he throws off all disguises. For the first and last time, he utters his prolonged, pathetic plaint of boredom, disillusionment, weariness, and pain.

"I feel that the intoxication of being alone is stealing over me, the intoxication of sweet repose which nothing will disturb. . . . I cannot be called, invited or taken anywhere; I cannot be oppressed by smiles or harassed by polite attentions. I am alone, really alone, and really free." At Cannes he is reminded of his sad fate as a celebrity. "Whoever keeps a *salon* must be able to produce celebrities, and a hunt is organized to procure them. . . . The woman who feels this strange desire to have a man of letters at her home, as one might have a parrot whose talk attracts the concierges of the neighbourhood, may choose between poets and novelists. Poets are greater idealists, novelists are more unexpected. Poets are more sentimental, novelists more

practical. It is a matter of taste and temperament.
. . . But the novelist is more dangerous than the poet.
He ransacks, pillages, and exploits everything that
comes before his eyes. One can never be at ease with
him, never sure that he will not strip one naked some
day between the sheets of his book." And with sardonic
humour he pictures the process of becoming a literary
lion, the idol of a *salon*, "out of which one comes with
the feeling of having been in a church."

He has visions of the conversations, of the ideas,
which pass for entertaining, "ineluctable proofs of the
eternal, universal, indestructible, and omnipotent stupidity" of the human race. "All this conception of
God, of the clumsy divinity who fails, then tries again,
to create the first beings, who listens to our confidences
and notes them down, of a god who is a policeman, a
Jesuit, a lawyer, a a gardener, dressed in a uniform, in a
gown, in wooden clogs. Then their denials of God based
on human logic, the arguments for and against, the history of sacred beliefs, of schisms, of heresies, of philoso-
phies, of affirmations that are doubts, the puerility of
principles, the ferocious and bloody violence of the mak-
ers of hypotheses, the chaos of reputations, the entire
miserable effort of this wretched, impotent creature to
conceive or to divine an idea, to know something, and so
ready to believe — all go to prove that he was sent into
this little world solely to eat, drink, produce children
and songs, and to murder his neighbour by way of recre-
ation."

"Blessed are those whom life satisfies, who are
amused, who are happy . . . But there are others who,
exhausting in a flash of thought the brief gamut of
possible satisfactions, remain crushed by the nullity of
happiness, the monotony and poverty of terrestrial
pleasures. By the time they are thirty, all is over for

them. What could they expect? Nothing entertains them any more. They have made the round of our feeble joys. Blessed are those who do not feel the abominable nausea of always repeating the same actions; blessed are those who have the courage to begin each day afresh the same tasks. . . . Blessed are those who do not discover with immense disgust that nothing changes, that nothing passes, that everything tires. . . .

"Cannot people see that we are always imprisoned within ourselves, and never succeed in escaping, condemned to drag the ball and chain of our leaden dreams? The only progress of our mental effort consists in tabulating material facts by means of ridiculously imperfect instruments. Our diseases come from microbes, but where do the microbes come from? . . . We are ignorant, blind, and powerless; we guess nothing, we imagine nothing. We are shut up and imprisoned within ourselves. Yet, people marvel at the genius of man!"

As he sails the Mediterranean the emptiness of life seems all the more profound when contrasted with the loveliness of nature — of the sea above all, which is feminine in its elusive cruelty and charm. Art and literature are vain repetitions. Even war and patriotism, about which he held forth so respectfully to Zola, now inspire him to pages of anti-militaristic denunciation. He arrives at a platitude, pardonable in a man who rarely used his brains to manipulate ideas: If the people would turn their weapons against the governments that drive them to massacre, there would be an end to war. . . . "But that day will never come!"

There are moments of respite, when illusion is reborn. "There are days, it is true, when I feel the horror of existence so much that I wish to die. I experience a feeling of intense suffering at the endless monotony of the landscape, of people, of ideas. I am astonished and revolted by the mediocrity of the universe, the pettiness of all things fills me with disgust, the poverty of human nature overpowers me. On the contrary, there are other days when I enjoy life like an animal. If my restless, tormented mind, exhausted by work, soars to hopes which are not of this world, and then falls back into a contempt for everything, having proved its nullity, my animal body drinks in the intoxication of life. I love the sky like a bird, the forests like a roaming wolf, the mountain crags like a chamois; I like to roll in the deep grass and run on it like a horse, to swim in the clear waters like a fish. I feel stirring within me something of all the animal species, of all the instincts and confused desires of the inferior creatures. I love the earth as they do, not as you human beings do. . . . When it is fine, as it is to-day, I feel in my veins the blood of the ancient fauns, lascivious wanderers. I am no longer a man amongst men, but at one with all creatures and all things."

The sequel to this mood is, of course, the awakening of desire for woman, under the moonlight; and appropriate references to Victor Hugo and Apuleius. Two days later he has a more typical night to record:

"As soon as I lay down, I knew I should not sleep. I remained on my back, with my eyes closed, my brain awake, and my nerves on edge. . . . Suddenly something creaked. . . . . The soft, dolorous, plaintive tone of this noise made my flesh quiver. Then, nothing; an infinite silence; . . . suddenly the unrecognizable, delicate wail began again. As I listened to it, I felt as if a jagged blade were sawing my heart. . . . I waited attentively and heard it again, this sound which seemed to come from myself . . . or rather, which resounded within me like a secret, profound, and desolate call! Yes, it was a cruel voice, a voice I knew and expected,

which drove me to desperation. This curious, faint
sound passed over me, sowing the seeds of terror and
delirium. . . . It was the voice that cries incessantly
to our souls, making continual reproaches, obscurely
and painfully; a voice that is torturing, maddening,
mysterious, unappeasable, unforgettable, and ferocious,
reproaching us with the things we have done and those
we have left undone, the voice of vague remorse, of
irrevocable regrets, of days that are gone, of women who
might, perhaps, have loved us, of forgotten things, of
vain joys, of dead hopes; the voice of what is temporary, elusive, deceptive, and ephemeral, of what we did
not and never shall achieve, the frail little voice which
proclaims the abortion of life, the futility of effort, the
powerlessness of the mind, and the weakness of the
flesh.

"Alas, I have desired all things and enjoyed nothing.
I should have been endowed with the vitality of an
entire race, with the diverse intelligence that is scattered amongst all men, with all the faculties, all the
strength, and a thousand existences in reserve, but I am
reduced to watching everything and taking nothing.
. . . How I wish, at times, that I could stop thinking
and feeling, that I could live like an animal in a bright,
warm country, in a yellow land without crude and brutal
greens, in an Oriental country, where sleep is joyful and
one awakes without sorrow . . . where love is not
fraught with anguish. . . ."

This insomnia, culminating in the inevitable dream of
sunshine and lazy pleasure, calms his spirit. "I shall
have four or five wives in quiet, noiseless apartments,
wives chosen from the five continents of the world, who
will bring me the savour of feminine beauty as it has
blossomed in all races." But now his body aches. "I
was seized by the pains in my head, the horrible afflic-

tion, the headache which is worse than any torture, pounding one's brain, driving to madness, scattering ideas, and destroying memory, as the wind drives the dust before it. I had to lie down in my cabin with a bottle of ether to my nostrils.

"First there was a sort of mental torpor, a sense of sleepy well-being. . . . Soon the curious and charming sensation of emptiness in my breast extended to my arm and legs, which became light . . . as if flesh and bone had melted. . . . I no longer suffered. . . . And I heard voices, four voices, two dialogues, without understanding the words. . . . But I realized that this was merely an increased buzzing in my ears. I was not asleep; I was awake; I could understand, feel, and reason with extraordinary clarity, profundity, and power. . . . It was not the dream that comes from hashish, nor the sickly visions of opium. It was a prodigious acuteness of the reasoning faculties, a new way of seeing, judging, and appreciating men and matters, with the certainty, an absolute consciousness, that this way was the right way. . . . I suddenly recalled the old image of the Scriptures, and I felt I had tasted of the Tree of Knowledge."

The diary goes on, reflecting present fears and past. He recalls the slavery of the petty employé, who has neither the freedom nor the comparative wealth of the artisan, and bitter memories of the Ministry of Marine come back to him. He looks at the crowd in front of a church at Saint-Raphaël, and dwells at length upon the grotesque ugliness of the human body. His phobia of crowds becomes more and more pronounced. "I cannot go to a theatre or a public fête. I at once feel strangely, unbearably ill at ease, a horrible sense of irritation." He tries to justify this fear by the usual commonplace about the herd instinct, but the receipt of letters at Saint-Tropez provokes him to comments which show that people, even singly, are obnoxious to him. "Let nobody become attached to me. Will nobody ever understand affection without coupling with it some id⟨ a of possession and despotism? . . . No sooner has one smiled at some stranger's politeness than the latter acquires rights over one, asks what one is doing, and accuses one of neglect."

One subject can still soften his misanthropy. The author of the early stories shows through, for once, in his last sustained hymn to the goddess who treated him so well and so cruelly. France, he insists, is the only country where gallantry is really understood:

"He who guards in his heart the gallant flame of past centuries surrounds women with a tenderness that is deep, soft, moving, and alert at the same time. He loves everything belonging to them, everything that comes from them, everything they are, and everything they do. He likes their clothes, their knickknacks, their ornaments, their cunning, their ingenuousness, their perfidy, their lies, and their pretty ways. He loves them all, rich and poor, young and old, dark and fair, plump and slender. He feels happy near them or in their midst. He can stay there indefinitely, without being tired or bored, happy in their mere presence.

"By his very first words, a look, a smile, he knows how to show that he loves them, to arouse their attention, to stimulate their desire to please, to make them employ all their powers of seduction. . . . He can tell them what they like to hear, make them understand his thoughts; and, without ever shocking them, without ever offending their frail and unstable modesty, he can let them see in his eyes keen but veiled desire, ever awake, trembling on his lips, always burning in his veins. He is their friend and their slave, the servant of

their caprices and the admirer of their bodies. . . . In
the street he loves the passing woman whose glance
touches him. He loves the little girl whose hair is down
her back, who has a blue ribbon in it and a flower on her
breast. . . . He loves the unknown women against
whom he brushes, the little shopkeeper dreaming in her
doorway, the languid beauty lolling in her open carriage."

All his friends have testified to his preference for female society, his inability to make himself interesting
to men, his cold politeness to his own sex, and his way
of closing up like an oyster if another man joined his
conversation with a woman. Now he confesses that
"as soon as he is in the presence of a woman, his heart
is moved and his mind is alert. He thinks of her, talks
for her, tries to please her, and to make her realize that
she pleases him. Tender words spring to his lips; his
eyes caress; he longs to kiss her hand, to touch her
dress. For him women embellish the world and make
life seductive. He likes to sit at their feet, for the sole
pleasure of being there. He likes to meet their eyes
simply to look for their fugitive and veiled thoughts.
He likes to listen to their voices solely because they are
women's voices."

From all of which Maupassant deduces that Frenchmen, alone of their sex, have learned to be witty — a
point upon which one would like to have heard Marie
Bashkirtseff's comment.

CHAPTER IX

THE THUNDERBOLT

N THE spring of 1888 he had begun *Fort comme la mort*, but found it very difficult, "there are so many fine shades, things suggested rather than said." It is one of the most frequently corrected and revised of all his manuscripts, showing laborious effort and uncertainty as to form and design. Often only eight lines to a page survive without corrections, and twenty-six pages describing the death of Olivier Bertin were substituted for the first version of this scene before the story was published in book form. A full year elapsed between its conception and its appearance in *La Revue Illustrée*. Hélène Lecomte du Nouy had given Maupassant the subject, which Bourget had mentioned to her, and which he himself afterwards developed, in his own manner, as *Le Fantôme*.

The book is very definitely a part of Maupassant's final literary incarnation when, racked with pain and conscious that something irrevocable had happened, he tried to express the artificial, unfamiliar fashionable world in which his lot was now ironically cast. In *Fort comme la mort* he betrays his uncertainty of himself. "I wonder if I am not ill, I am so deeply disgusted by what I have been doing for so long with a certain pleasure, or with resigned indifference. . . . My mind is empty, my eyes are empty, my hands are empty. . . . This vain effort to work is exasperating. . . . What is it? Fatigue of the eyes or of the brain, exhaustion of the

creative faculty or an affection of the optic nerve?'
In his letters he writes: "It is curious how I am becoming mentally a different man from what I used to be.
I see it as I observe myself thinking of stories, discover-
ing and developing them, sounding and analysing the
imaginary people who come into my dreams. I get the
same pleasure from certain dreams, certain exaltations,
as I used to experience when I rowed madly in the sun."

Maupassant's indifference is gone; he is sentimental;
he forgets his reiterated philosophy of sex and shows the
reversal of the rôles, in which the man, grown older and
lonelier, sees his happiness destroyed by the woman.
His personal reflections are dragged in without being
particularly appropriate to the moment, as in the denunciation of the sterile heartlessness of society in *Fort
comme la mort*. Olivier Bertin, André Mariolle, and
Gaston de Lamarthe become simply reflections of the
author; they are neither transposed from observation
of others nor set down as types. Describing Madame
Guilleroy's dread of old age he confesses: "At this
moment I share her fears. I am depressed by the sight
of my grey hairs, my wrinkles, my faded cheeks, the
visible wearing away of the human body." He is obsessed by his own miseries; he is no longer at home in
his own world. The last two novels, diffuse and faltering, describe clearly only one character, and that character is Guy de Maupassant.

On his return from a trip to Africa early in 1889 Edmond de Goncourt met him at Princess Mathilde's, and
found him "animated, lively, and talkative. His
thinned and sunburned face made him less common-
looking than usual," he added characteristically. Solitude could not save him, nor such rests as this and his
Mediterranean trips afforded. He had to go off again,
and he wrote to his mother from Gérardmer, in the

Vosges: "I have had rheumatic pains, but after four days my stomach got much better. My legs recovered their elasticity, although I had cramps in my hands and shoulders. No sooner have I got back to Étretat than my headaches have come on again; I am weak and a mass of nerves. Work is absolutely impossible. When I write ten lines, I forget what I am at, and my thoughts float away as though through a sieve." He went one evening in September to Bougival to dine with Céard and had an epileptic fit, of which he had no recollection the next morning. Early in 1889 he gave *La Main gauche* to Ollendorff. Not a story in the book belonged to the previous year, and the general quality of those collected from his output of 1887, and of the half-dozen more recent tales, suggests that, if he was not self-critical when he described them as being of "the left hand," he might well have been. However, apparently the title was determined by the number of stories dealing with illegitimacy.

Dr. Sollier noted that year a return of the phenomenon described five years earlier in *Lui?* "As he was sitting at his table in the study, he thought he heard the door open. His servant had orders never to allow anybody in while he was writing. Maupassant turned around, and was not a little astonished to see himself enter, sit down in front of him, with his face in his hands, and begin to dictate exactly what he was writing. When he had finished and he stood up, the hallucination disappeared."

He tried his flat in Paris, but the noise had got on his tired nerves. Since *Fort comme la mort* had appeared, young writers were besieging him for advice, much to his annoyance. Ether and antipyrine gave some relief to his headaches, but days of work were lost, and his eyes had become so tender that the windows were heavily shaded with green blinds. It was so dark that François had to grope his way about. Étretat does not seem to help him much. Instead of cold douches, he tried bathing in the Seine, and this also failed to give him relief. He was put on various diets and anxiously consulted specialists, oculists in particular, but very naturally their advice had little effect upon his general condition. His nervous state was such that he was terribly upset by a few little spiders in his room and prepared an offensive against them as though his house were threatened by some fearful visitation.

With all these interruptions, there came others. A visit from a troop of Arabs who drank unaccustomed quantities of alcohol and performed the *danse du ventre*. They had come to Paris for the Exhibition of 1889, and Maupassant engaged them to dance for his friends. "It was a species of demoniacal revel. . . . We were too close. The actors were having more fun than the spectators," the indignant François said, having with much difficulty escaped the embraces of one of the dancers. An English nobleman also appeared, and was shown the house at Fécamp which was Madame Tellier's. He recognized it at once, much to Maupassant's delight, for the actual house he had described in the story was at Rouen. There was also a box of dolls which Maupassant returned to the lady who sent them, after he had ripped them open in front and stuffed them with rags to represent the increased bulk with which circumstances may endow the female sex. The younger Dumas, a Princess, and various wild women of high station likewise descended upon the rue Montchanin, talked bawdry, and caused François' Master much embarrassment.

At Étretat, however, he worked painfully, in all senses of the word, at the novel which was to be his last, *Notre*

Cœur, and on the 18th of August the anniversary of
Saint Helena was celebrated at La Guillette in a manner
which brought spectators flocking around the villa. The
trees were hung with flags and Chinese lanterns, and
musicians dressed in peasant smocks and high hats sat
upon barrels and supplied music for the country dances.
The garden and adjoining fields were crowded with
pretty ladies in bright costumes, and screams of laughter
echoed as far as the church where "the English who re-
side in Étretat can be heard singing like angels." Madame Lecomte du Nouy looked after the refreshment
tables, her artistic head looking beautiful, as Maupassant said, "standing out against a background of flowers
specially arranged with that intention." A young lady
won a cock in a raffle, and Madame Plessy Arnould a
live rabbit. But the great event of the day was the
drama performed in a dark alley of trees:

"A policeman is seen in a great state of agitation beside the body of a perfectly naked woman, who is hanging by her feet. His ambition, it seems, is to experience
a new sensation. In the presence of the astounded
guests he plunges a knife into her stomach and the blood
spurts out." This terrible realism, aided by the half-
light, caused the utmost consternation. Then the mur-
derer is arrested and put into prison, which he sets on
fire. In vain the firemen try to extinguish the blaze.
The prison is made of wood and straw, soaked in parra-
fin oil, and real flames roar, while the firemen, unable to
put them out, turn their hoses on the crowd. — Thus,
with the help of a crudely painted canvas curtain and
some blood from the butcher's, Maupassant gave his
friends a foretaste of the Grand Guignol.

It was the last scene of happiness for him at La Guillette, that afternoon in August, when Massenet played
parts of his as yet unpublished *Werther*, and Maupas-

sant's friends gathered to an entertainment which had its beginnings in the amateur theatricals that were a part of his earliest memories of home in Normandy. It was, indeed, his farewell to the place of which he was so fond, and to the Norman countryside which held every memory that he really loved, and which had inspired all that was truest and most enduring in his work. Soon the cold came, and the winds blew mournfully around the villa, where his fire was never to be extinguished, but they no longer charmed his melancholy or stirred his blood as he walked along the cliffs. A park was planned on the site beside his, and he tried without success to sell his property for that purpose. In November 1889, his brother Hervé died of general paralysis, and Maupassant, at least, was not deceived by his mother's theory that this was due to sunstroke.

He avoided Goncourt's gatherings, knowing that entries were being made in the famous *Journal* which would hardly be to his credit, for his eccentricities were becoming noticeable in Paris. He moved from the rue Montchanin to a flat over a baker's shop in the Avenue Victor Hugo, where the noise all night was, of course, intolerable. Whereupon he threatened a lawsuit for damages, on account of the cost of moving, and loss of work and rest, unless the lease was cancelled. Léon Daudet, as yet merely an unpublished young author, without his subsequently and strangely acquired respect for the Throne and the Altar, listened to the gossip in his father's circle and heard many strange tales: that Maupassant had borrowed an illustrated edition of the works of de Sade, in order to broaden the horizon of a young servant girl "with great aptitudes for debauchery"; that he had asked a lady who was dining with him to crawl in her chemise, on all fours, around the table; and much more to that effect. "It was evident

to the naked eye that there were three Maupassants, a
fine writer, a perfect ass, and a very sick man."

It was the first of these three who had said: "Three
things dishonour an author: the *Revue des Deux Mondes*,
the decoration of the Legion of Honour, and the French
Academy." It was chiefly the second who struggled
over the *Notre Cœur*, the final reflection of the author
as the great lover of fashionable ladies; and it is generally the third who is held responsible for his unac-
countable surrender to the *Revue des Deux Mondes* in
1890, exactly ten years after the editor's refusal to print
La dernière escapade. The review made an arrange-
ment with him this year to have the first refusal of all
work, guaranteeing a minimum of twenty-two thousand, five hundred francs, at the rate of fifteen hundred
francs per printed sheet. This was a considerable sum,
and for it Maupassant laboured at the most frequently
erased and revised of all his manuscripts.

In the early part of the year he went to Cannes, and
in the summer he moved to the rue Boccador, where he
had five rooms facing South, with sunlight, a bathroom
with a shower-bath, a fencing-room, and the dubious
prospect of the recently erected Eiffel Tower. Everything seemed to be propitious for work once more, but
Maupassant's working days were now numbered. At
the beginning of the year, Havard had pressed him for
the title of his forthcoming book of stories, as he wanted
to do some advertising in advance, and he had rejected
Le Champ d'oliviers as unattractive, from a bookselling
standpoint. Finally, after some debate, Maupassant
hit upon *L'Inutile beauté*, the title of the second last
story he ever wrote, and this was taken for the volume,
which appeared in April.

In order to make up a book of the required length, the
author had again been obliged to go back, this time as

far as 1886. But he wrote four stories in 1890 for the
volume: *Le Champ d'oliviers*, which he read to Taine,
who thought it Æschylean; *Mouche*, his ultimate glance
into the happy past, with Léon Fontaine, Pinchon,
Albert de Joinville, and the boating-girls; *L'Inutile
beauté*, "a hundred times superior to *Le Champ d'oliviers*," as the author wrote to Havard, "the rarest story
I have ever written. Don't forget your excitement over
Mont-Oriol, which I never liked, and which is not worth
much. Send me the page proofs as quickly as possible.
My eyes are very bad and I am correcting very slowly."

Havard preferred *Le Champ d'oliviers*, as he declared
in his appreciation of this book, which was not only the
last he was ever to publish of Maupassant's, but which
also marked the end of their pleasant relationship. "It
is a sheer masterpiece. In my opinion you have never
done anything finer. It is Maupassant in the plenitude
of his prodigious talent. When it has been the lot of a
publisher to savour such a morsel, if he has an instinct
for the beautiful and for great art, he cannot help feeling
profoundly moved, even if he be just a paper-merchant.
But it sometimes makes his duty painful, for he can read
nothing else afterwards."

Whatever Havard's deficiencies may have been, he
certainly knew how to write to his best-selling author,
and although Maupassant may have received more
tangible advantages from other publishers, none could
ever have surpassed, and few equalled, Havard as an
articulate believer in the adage: There is nothing like
leather. However, at this moment Maupassant's exasperation was at its height. He was fighting with his
landlord in the Avenue Victor Hugo, and he seems to
have tried to make a break with all his old editorial ties.
Meeting Huysmans in the street, he heard that Charpentier was bringing out an edition of *Les Soirées de*

Médan illustrated with the author's portraits, and he became hysterical. It was an outrage to publish an author's photograph; he had refused absolutely "to allow any photograph of himself to be taken, exhibited, or sold"; and he demanded the destruction of his portrait in all the copies that were in stock, or that could be recalled. The six have continued to adorn this edition for many years, but the outburst is characteristic of Maupassant's morbid fear of all revelations concerning his personality, which resulted in the bowdlerization or suppression of the few documents that survived his mother's anxiety lest any complete account of his career should be made after his death.

He was passing, at this time, through the last stage of his mental disintegration, and his account of it appeared on the 6th of April, 1890, in the *Echo de Paris*. As in *Lui?* and *Le Horla*, the phenomenon described in *Qui sait?* is preceded by "that mysterious presentiment which possesses us when we are about to witness the inexplicable." The victim comes home at night, hears strange noises of footsteps that are not human, a rustling and rumbling, the tapping of "wooden and iron crutches vibrating like cymbals," and he sees his furniture marching in ghostly procession out of the house. He believes it is merely an hallucination, but next day he learns that his furniture has all been removed. In an anguish of mortal fear he goes through the motions of reporting a robbery. "If I had told them what I knew . . . if I had, . . . they would have locked me up, not the thieves." His nervous state is deplorable. The doctors order rest and change. He travels to Genoa, Venice, Florence, Rome, Naples, Sicily, and Northern Africa, and returns with "that curious impression of the sick man who believes he is cured, but who is warned by a secret pain that the root of the illness has not been extirpated." One day, in a sinister side street of Rouen he sees all his things in an antiquity shop, under the charge of a hideous old sorcerer, completely bald, with a scraggy, yellowish beard, and a "wrinkled, swollen face in which the eyes are invisible." When the police try to find and arrest this man, he and the furniture have disappeared. Then the servant notifies his master that all the things have been brought back as mysteriously as they were taken away. But now the owner's terror is complete. He cannot tell what he knows; he dares not live again with that furniture, "as though nothing had happened, but haunted by the fear lest something similar should occur again." He goes to an insane asylum and asks to be interned, to be cut off from all his friends. But, even prisons and asylums are not safe.

The parallels between the three stories, *Lui?*, *Le Horla*, and *Qui sait?* and the conditions of Maupassant's own derangement are as obvious as the differences between the three stages of hallucination described. The remedy for his fear of autoscopy in *Lui?* is companionship at night; for his fear of the Horla the remedy is travel, flight, then suicide. Finally, he renounces even that solution, and prefers the escape provided by being declared insane. In the first two stages, the victim resists his hallucinations, which, in lucid moments, he knows for what they are. In *Qui sait?* he is passive; he has passed beyond normal mental conditions and has surrendered to his insane obsession. His supreme act of sanity is to give himself up as mad.

Such was the last story written and published by Maupassant. It was not noticed amidst the discussion of *Le Champ d'oliviers* and *L'Inutile beauté*, but it is the most significant thing in the volume which came out that spring. *Notre Cœur* was running then in the *Revue des Deux Mondes*, and the author was assuring his mother that it "looked as if it were going to be a success. . . . Its novelty is a surprise and I have good hopes for it." In July, however, he was less satisfied, because all the discussion had centred in its appearance in the review, and people had stopped talking about it when the book came out. He thought it would sell better than *Fort comme la mort*, but finally admitted that there were practically no sales at all, despite the great success of the book. "The reason is that the *Revue des Deux Mondes* has taken away the purchasers amongst the best society in Paris, and amongst the official people, the lawyers and teachers, in the provincial towns." However, he has revised his opinion of the *Revue*, where, "on general principles, it has been an excellent thing for *Notre Cœur*" to appear. "The special public of this periodical now knows me and will buy me later on. I have gained new readers."

After restless wanderings to Aix-les-Bains, Cannes, Nice, and to Algeria, once more he returns to Paris. This time it has done him little good to take refuge in the sun. The port of Algiers he finds as noisy as the Avenue Victor Hugo, and Allouma and Marocca no longer tempt him. "We dined at M. Tirman's; his court and palace made me think of an African King of Yvetot . . . The ladies of the establishment were two in number. One felt no desire to increase their families. My neighbour was a Baronne, jaundiced, hysterical, and scraggy, with her dress cut so low in the back one could see her legs. The relative modesty of the front was a sign of prudence rather than of prudery." They went from hotel to hotel "groaning over the rooms and the food." Africa, too, had lost its charm.

Towards the end of November Goncourt met him in the train with Zola, Céard, Mirbeau, and others who were going down to Rouen for the inauguration of the

Flaubert monument. "I was struck this morning by the unhealthy appearance of Maupassant, his haggard face, his brick-red complexion . . . by the glassy stare in his eyes. He does not look as if he would live long." This was his last reunion with the remnants of the group that had seen him rise to a popularity and famie wth which Zola's, alone of that circle, could compare. As they passed along by the Seine his thoughts dwelt upon that river and all it had meant to him, for good and ill. "It was my rowing there," he said, stretching out his arm, "which has brought me to the state in which I am to-day." After the ceremony, at which Céard and Goncourt made up their quarrel, "united by Flaubert's shade," they drank and dined and talked of old times. Even *La Maison turque* was recalled. But Maupassant had not joined them. After having held out hopes of a lunch on the way down from Paris, he had slipped away by himself to see a relative.

His malady now follows its relentless course, punctuated by attacks of megalomania and persecution mania, by periods of febrile excitement and complete collapse. For long intervals his mind is clear and permitted by malign fate to realize with the acuteness of desperation what is happening. When preparing his travel sketches for *La Vie errante* he burned nearly all the section on Italy in a rage against the politics of Crispi; because *La Maison Tellier* was allowed to go out of print, he broke with Havard completely, although the latter reprinted the book at once when called upon to do so. Money comes in and he omits to draw upon it, and then demands an accounting. From Cannes he utters despairing appeals. "The sun is streaming in through my windows and it is so warm. Why can I not completely share in this sense of well-being?" If he could howl like the dogs which increase his nightly melancholy, he would do so. "I think it might relieve me to howl for hours at a time in the darkness."

Jacques Normand had seen dramatic possibilities in *L'Enfant*, a story from *Clair de lune*, and they had made it into a play which was produced at the Gymnase Theatre on the 4th of March, 1891, under the title of *Musotte*. It had required all the diplomacy of Ollendorff and other friends to prevent Maupassant from upsetting everything. "Maupassant was very nervous and irritable and did not often come " to the rehearsals. He took a violent dislike to the producer, and when the dress rehearsal took place, the play did not make a good impression, the performers being discouraged and the audience only mildly interested.

On the opening night Maupassant and his collaborator sat in the stage box, where he cowered behind the lattice shutter, murmuring: "Oh, that light! that light! It burns my eyes." According to Normand, "the audience applauded enthusiastically, and we could see by their faces that they were moved. Maupassant certainly was pleased by a success far greater than we had expected. But his joy was silent. . . . After the performance we shook hands outside, in the Boulevard Bonne Nouvelle, and went our separate ways. I watched him disappear into the night, into the middle of the crowd, walking with his solid stride, with a slight roll, like a sailor's." With his head down and his collar turned up, he disappeared. When his next play was produced, *La paix du ménage*, in 1893, he was worse than dead, and was far beyond participation in either its financial or literary success.

Like Henry James he turned to the theatre only as a means of making money, and none of his plays shows any real dramatic talent. He talked much of dramatizing his stories, at this time particularly, but no longer

of writing an original play.   He had a long conversation
the day after *Musotte* opened, in which he boasted to
Normand of all that he could do for the theatre, but
denounced hysterically the Reading Committee of the
Comédie Française, saying they would regret their rule
which would force him to bemean himself by submitting
a play to them before it was accepted.   It was Dumas
fils who actually went through this formality for *La paix
du ménage*.   "Plays?   Why, I can write as many of them
as I want," he shouted.   "Think: in addition to my
novels, . . . which all contain a play in embryo, I
have written more than two hundred short stories, every
one of which provides a dramatic subject, a tragedy or
a comedy. . . . Two hundred stories. . . . Think of
it!"

His real attitude was somewhat different, as he admitted in the next breath.   "I really do not like the
theatre.   I go there very rarely.   It is uncomfortable.
Bad seats and bad air.   I positively cannot breathe.   As
for the play form, it is, in my opinion, an inferior form,
very remote from me.   I cannot believe in the reality of
fictitious beings represented by actors behind footlights,
in front of scenery made out of painted cardboard.
However, I will rejuvenate this old-fashioned thing.
On all sides I am asked to authorize plays drawn from
my works. . . . Just think . . . two hundred stories
. . . all mine . . . from which I can make comedies
or dramas, as I please . . .!"   And again he was
divagating.

The very next month, having promised to dramatize
Yvette for Albert Carré of the Vaudeville, he told the real
truth in a letter "There will be no *Yvette* this winter, and
there probably never will be any.   The theatre absolutely bores me.   I cannot bring myself to see other
people's plays, which is not calculated to give me cour-

age to start my own. . . . It is a dead art. Everything
that pleases and moves one in a novel . . . disappears
entirely in the theatre, owing to the need for exaggeration, and the necessity for working and embodying the
real persons one has seen in actors, irrespective of how
talented they may be." The fragment of *Yvette* as a
play found amongst his papers indicated that Maupassant was wiser and Carré luckier than the latter doubtless supposed.

This spring he suffered greatly from neuralgic pains,
but he believed his eyes and head were simply "greatly
fatigued after this abominable winter, which has left
me like a frozen plant." He adds a new specialist to
his collection and, of course, announces comforting
generalities upon which illusion may seize. "I have
consulted about my nervous condition a man who is
supposed to be far superior to Charcot. . . . He examined me at great length and listened to my whole story."
And he is gravely informed that he is just suffering from
"overstrain," that "most writers and stockbrokers are
in the same state." Once more Maupassant is advised
to diet, to take cold douches, to lead a quiet life, to
spend the summer in a warm climate. "I am not un-
easy about you," concluded the celebrated Dr. Dejerine.

The eminent scientist who was so superior to Charcot
in Maupassant's estimation was not very happily inspired, it would seem, for in June Maupassant wrote
the last long letter preserved by his mother, and it is a
lamentable document. He had gone to Divonne to a
sanitorium with which he was familiar, and he assured
her the cold douches had made him "put on fat and
muscle." Taine had suggested he should come to
Champel, near Geneva, where "he was cured of an illness just like mine in forty days," and Maupassant
proposed to leave immediately. The letter is written by

a faltering hand and mind; misspellings, blots, mistakes
in grammar, and laboured penmanship are its outstand-
ing characteristics. And the mother is invited in a post-
cript to "notice how this letter is written with a firmer
hand."

Jean Lahor, the poet, professionally known as Dr. Ca-
zalis, met Maupassant at Geneva. When they arrived
at Champel, the latter called on his friend Dorchain —
whose name he could not manipulate in the last letter —
and at once explained that he had left Divonne because
the Lake of Geneva had overflowed and flooded his
room, and his douches were not cold enough! He displayed an umbrella which, he said, could be found only
in a place known to him. "I have had more than three
hundred of them sold to people in Princess Mathilde's
circle." He had a stick with which he had defended
himself against three mad dogs behind him and three
bullies in front of him. He whispered in Dorchain's ear
about a marvellous young lady in Geneva and boasted
of what she had enabled him to do. They persuaded
Maupassant that Dorchain had been cured by the treatment, after suffering from exactly the same symptoms.
This pious lie helped to calm him, and one day he produced a brief-case full of papers and showed the first
fifty pages of his unfinished novel, *L'Angélus*. "I have
not been able to write another page of it for a year. If
the book is not finished in three months, I will kill myself." One night he read the fragment to his friends,
and when he had done, he wept. He never finished the
manuscript, but it was no fault of his that his threat was
not carried out.

When he left Champel for Cannes in September he
had one of his deceptive interludes, and telegraphed to
his mother in Nice, reassuring her about his health and
promising to come to see her in October. He even

planned to write his long-postponed article on Turgenev
and asked her to reread the books and give him memo-
randa. Then he departed for Paris to "drink a goblet
of social life for three weeks," before settling down to
work. What drew him to Paris, François has explained.
"On the 20th of September, at two in the afternoon, the
electric bell . . . rings in an uncertain way. I open
the door and find myself face to face with the woman
who already done such harm to my master. As usual,
she passes me stiffly and enters the drawing-room, her
marble countenance showing not the slightest change.
. . . Ought I not to warn this fatal visitor, reproach
her with the crime she is so unconcernedly committing,
put her out without ceremony? . . . Since my master
consents to receive her, I can only bow to her. . . . I
may now confess how deeply I regret not having had the
courage to send that *vampire* away! My master would
still be living. . . . In the evening he seems tired and
does not mention the visit."

Maupassant had never discussed this unknown lady
of Jewish origin, the heroine of *Notre Cœur*, whose
husband's susceptibilities had to be spared. When
François first saw her, just before that novel was published, he thought "she is not of the *demi-monde*, but
too much perfumed; nor does she belong to that most
distinguished set where they like to laugh and by which
master is so much invited. She is of the middle-class
but of good taste and resembles the great ladies who
have been educated at the Convent of *Les Oiseaux* or *Le
Sacré Cœur*. She has the well-bred, or even severe,
manners of those places. . . . She is remarkably beautiful and wears with supreme smartness her tailor-made
costumes, either pearl-grey or dark grey, with a waist-
band of real gold tissue. Her hats are very simple,
matching her dress."

preme moment, before he returned to Passy, not for her, but on a quest which even then she barely guessed. The events of that night had no witnesses except the two women, from whom nothing was afterwards heard except a telegram. While his brain was dying his heroine had fled in terror, "as a child, who has stifled its pet bird with kisses, hides to watch it die."

After that eternal good-bye, Maupassant went back to Cannes, and promised to spend New Year's Day with his mother. When the day came, he felt so ill that he dreaded to show himself to her. He was persuaded to go by his servant, and on his arrival his mother noticed nothing abnormal until they sat down to dinner. Then he began to talk of swallowing a pill which had told him of an event in which he was interested. His mind was wandering; he noticed the grief and astonishment on the faces about him, and relapsed into silence. His mother wanted him to stay with her at Nice, but he ordered his carriage, said good-bye, and drove back to Cannes.

Now he was at the final point of a crisis which he had more than once analysed. He had told Heredia only a few weeks before that he would not outlive his mind. "I came into literature like a meteor, I will go out of it like a thunderbolt." As he had once said to his doctor: "There is no room for hesitation between madness and death." The time had now come to choose death. After François had left him more or less quiet in bed, he utilized this final lucid interval. He tried to shoot himself, but François had emptied his revolver. He tried to cut his throat, but could only wound it with a steel paper-knife.

They bound up his throat, and he was pale and calm, as though nothing more could touch him. For two days he was thus abstracted; then suddenly he revealed

what had become of him. "François, are you ready?
War is declared! Why do you delay? Now is the time
to hurry." At length his reason was extinguished. He
became violent and was put in a strait-jacket. They
took him down in that garment to the sea, hoping that
the sight of his yacht might stir some chord of memory.
His glassy stare relaxed, and he gazed long and tenderly
at his beloved boat. His lips moved, but he could not
speak, and while he looked back several times, they
took him away.

François saw a telegram which had come on that first
tragic night of the new year, and had since been opened.
It contained love and good wishes from the heroine of
Notre Cœur.

CHAPTER X

APOTHEOSIS

N JANUARY the 7th, 1892, his publisher, Ollendorff, and Jean Lahor met Maupassant at the Gare de Lyon, where he arrived in charge of François and an attendant who had been sent from the asylum at Passy. He was taken to that establishment, which he never left until the day of his death. From this point onwards his body was in the care of his keepers and his reputation was abandoned to the rumours of friends and enemies. The news of his attempted suicide was public, but gradually the memory of him lingered only in the circle of his friends.

At Princess Mathilde's they had news of him from Dr. Blanche, and Goncourt's diary at length obtained the facts whose precursors Maupassant had so carefully kept out of that ruthless record of the times. "He still labours under the illusion that he has been salted. He is apathetic or irritable, and believes the doctors are persecuting him by waiting for him in the corridor and injecting him with morphine whose drops are burning holes in his brain. He has the fixed idea that he is being robbed, that his servant has stolen six thousand francs; in a few days the six thousand francs have become sixty thousand."

François, who stayed with him, shared for a while the illusion of the family that Maupassant would recover, but the flashes of lucidity grew fewer. One day his master accused the valet of having ousted him from the

Figaro, because he was writing to Madame de Maupassant. At other times he hankered after his study in the rue Boccador and his work, or sat with closed eyes composing verses. He had fits of megalomania and persecution mania, which were the constant elements in his insanity. He was fighting invisible enemies; he was filled with precious stones; he raved about millions of francs, during his delirious nights. As he wandered in the grounds his preoccupation with all forms of vegetation was noticeable, and when he planted a branch in one of the flower-beds he said, with a laugh, "next year we shall have little Maupassants." But on receiving grapes from Madame Lecomte du Nouy, he refused them with a bestial chuckle: "Why, they are made of copper!"

The author of *Amitié amoureuse* came several times, begging to be allowed to see him, but his mother jealously prohibited all visits from his women friends. No member of his family ever visited him, nor did his oldest friends, only those of his later years, Ollendorff, Henry Fouquier, the critic, and Cahen d'Anvers, the composer. By the autumn Maupassant could no longer recognize Dr. Blanche, and he had ceased to be interested in his callers. When Pol Arnault saw him after the New Year, he had been put into a strait-waistcoat and did not know his friend.

When *La Paix du ménage* was produced at the Comédie Française in March, with Worms and Le Bargy in the two men's parts and Mlle. Bartet as the woman, the critics were obviously influenced by what seemed like the visitation of a figure from beyond the grave. Sarcey even said prematurely "if Maupassant had lived," in explaining that there were the makings of a dramatist in the play. Fouquier praised it in the *Figaro,* obviously a personal tribute, but Sarcey, Lemaître, and the rest cautiously expressed their astonishment at the prepon-

derant influence of Dumas *fils* in this "Dumavaudage."
What they failed to notice was that here again, as in
Musotte, the piece was not written expressly for the
theatre. Its two acts were based on two stories, *Au bord
du lit*, which had appeared in *Gil Blas* as early as 1883,
and *Etrennes*, which was published in the same paper in
1887, and it is not improbable that Dumas *fils* had done
more to the script than merely act as its sponsor before
the Reading Committee. Maupassant's last reference
to it was in a letter to his mother, in 1890, where he
said: "I have just revised, or rather re-written, my
little play in one act, formerly in two, under the title of
La paix du foyer. I now think it is perfect, and I have
no doubts as to its success when a favourable opportunity occurs to produce it." This is obviously not the
play which demonstrated, once and for all, that Maupassant's talent for dramatic narrative did not make
him a dramatist.

Ollendorff published the volume of his plays, the closing volume of his work as Maupassant had prepared it
for publication. It was his mother who arranged the
posthumous works, defying in this his express wishes,
little to the advantage of his reputation, and in curious
contradiction to her fanatical zeal in carrying out his
other intentions, real or imaginary: the transference of
all his books from Havard, the destruction of biographical documents, the intimidation of all research, and the
confusion of the arrangements made for the manage-
ment of his estate.

Maupassant was now helpless and hopeless. He had
become "animalized," as Dr. Blanche told Goncourt.
At Easter he sat in the garden amidst the budding and
blossoming trees, and dreamed of the poplars in Normandy sighing in the west wind. He did not know that
a woman had come to their last *rendez-vous* in Passy.

From a distance she watched the shadow of her lover, "pale, aged, and weak, his features drawn, his eyes red-rimmed and lifeless, his flabby cheeks giving him the appearance of having jowls." His shoulders were bent as he brooded, but as a sob shook her, he seemed to hear a sound, and looked up in her direction, a puzzled and uncomprehending glance. "I kiss your feet that they may bring you to me without delay"; he had written, "I kiss your hands that are so white and your lips that are so red. . . . I want you so badly. . . ." Now she had come, as she had too often come before, only to return heart-broken to her memories and her letters.

On the 6th of July, 1893, he was dead, "extinguished like a lamp without oil." Like Olivier Bertin he lay, "relaxed, impassible, inanimate, indifferent to all misery, in the sudden peace of Eternal Oblivion," to quote the words which his fumbling pen had sought many times before they rhythmically closed *Fort comme la mort*.

Two days later he was buried in the Montparnasse Cemetery. Zola, Goncourt, all his friends were present, and Zola made the first speech of the many that were to be pronounced over him in later years. "Let him sleep the good sleep he so dearly purchased, confident in the triumphant health and sanity of the work he has left behind him! It will live and with it his name."

In 1895 his friends tried to transfer his remains to Père Lachaise near the grave of Alfred de Musset, but Madame de Maupassant would not consent, although the city of Paris had ceded the plot for that purpose. He continues to lie in the simple grave, his name only inscribed above his head, on a slab supported by two columns, between which stands an open book, at the base.

Two years later, however, the oratory prepared for

that occasion was heard, when the Maupassant monument was unveiled in the Parc Monceau, with speeches
by Zola and Henry Houssaye, and a recitation by Esther
Brandès of the Comédie Française. A lady, presumably
modelled after the fashionable type of the period, re-
clines upon a seat at the base of the pedestal supporting
a bust of Maupassant. She leans one elbow upon a
cushion, while her other arm hangs down, holding a
half-closed book. It is apparently a monument to the
author's readers, whom he used to watch in this park.
The French Society of Authors was responsible for the
idea, Raoul Verlet for its execution, and the Ministry of
Fine Arts for the blessing pronounced upon it by M.
Rambaud in person.

On the 27th of May, 1900, the more presentable
monument was raised in the Square Solferino at Rouen,
the joint work of Verlet and Bernier. A pensive head
and shoulders, set upon a granite column, decorated by
the symbolic branch of Norman apple blossoms. Catulle Mendès, Auguste Dorchain, Jacques Normand,
Léo Claretie, Henry Fouquier, and José Maria de Heredia were there, in a vast crowd, and Normandy
admired itself in the accomplishment of her most
distinguished writer since Flaubert — whose name re-
curred at appropriate intervals. Under the broiling sun
the speeches and ceremonies rolled on, the crowd somewhat disappointed because Heredia and Albert Sorel,
the two Academicians present, had not donned their
green uniforms. But, it was explained, they could not
do so because the illustrious deceased had not been one
of the Immortals. Military and local musicians reminded Rouen that Boïeldieu, too, had been one of
them. When Gaston Le Breton, on behalf of the Rouen
Committee, had offered the monument to the city, and
had contrived a friendly word for every living person

Monument to Guy de Maupassant at Rouen

connected with the affair, Heredia spoke at length and eloquently, and exclusively about the dead. He was followed by Pol Neveux, after Henry Fouquier and the Mayor had spoken, and these two friends of Maupassant succeeded, not only in making their hearers forget the usual rhetoric for such occasions, but also in giving a more vivid outline and a more discerning estimate of the author's career than any since. Mlle. Moréno of the Comédie Française recited three poems by Maupassant, *L'Oiseleur*, *Découverte*, and *Les Oies Sauvages*, and such was the grace of her art and the beauty of her voice that enthusiastic applause created, for a moment or two, the illusion that Maupassant was also a poet. Mlle. Brandès had not been so fortunate with Jacques Normand's effusion composed for the ceremony at the Parc Monceau.

His bust stands in the shady park, not far from the medallion of his master, Flaubert. This was the beginning of the apotheosis. While his family had feared that his work would bring in nothing after a year or so, his sales and his reputation grew. Madame Laure de Maupassant had tried to commit suicide in one of her hysterical crises; his father had vainly tried to introduce order into the chaos of family scenes and strife which flared up after Maupassant was gone, and the headstrong old lady had exerted all the authority of her son's affection for her, demonstrating that Guy and Hervé were not the only neurasthenics in the Maupassant household. Her elder son's life and work became her jealous monopoly and chief preoccupation, and all who tried to touch upon the subject had to submit to her rulings or risk excommunication. Madame Lecomte du Nouy never was forgiven for having dared to admit publicly her association and friendship with Maupassant.

His mother delivered the fragments of two novels, *L'Angélus* and *L'Ame étrangère*, and the posthumous volumes of early stories, *Le Colporteur*, *Le Père Milon*, and *Les Dimanches d'un Bourgeois de Paris*, for publication, and Ollendorff began to issue the first collected edition of Maupassant as the century closed. Naturalism was dead, if Zola still lived, and the author's name no longer conjured up the same visions as in the heroic days of 1880. In England, it is true, the curse of the Vizetelly prosecution hung over him, as it did over Zola. Isolated books were sold in side streets as pornography, and an English biographer, who had known him personally, was afraid to write a life of Maupassant, even in the nineties, because of his shady reputation. In America he was more fortunate in being sponsored by Lafcadio Hearn and Howells, when England looked askance at him.

In other countries he was soon a classic, becoming, with Alexandre Dumas, Victor Hugo, and Balzac, the most widely read and widely translated writer in modern French literature. His syntax has been studied by German philologists, and he has engaged the frequent attention of American Ph.D's. Even as a physiognomist a stout thesis holds him up for academic scrutiny. These are, doubtless, the kind of tribute which the beloved disciple of Flaubert might exact, but that title, of which he was once so proud, came to have little practical significance for Maupassant. Flaubert's influence on the younger writer waned each year after his death, and ceased with *Une Vie*, in 1883, the novel which has so constantly been contrasted with *Un Cœur simple*, although its debt to *L'Éducation sentimentale* is obviously much greater, Jeanne being the feminine counterpart of Flaubert's Frédéric, the frustrated product of "sentimental education." That fatal facility and triviality of epithet and phrase which Flaubert tried to check, as in his comments on *Désirs*, made itself felt immediately after the stories in *La Maison Tellier*.

The exigencies of frequent and rapid production soon produced those stereotyped settings, a group around the fire in the drawing-room, the men lingering over their wine and cigars, or the experience suggested by some chance remark, after which follows what is often nothing better than an anecdote or a newspaper report. The exact word is no longer sought and the strings of nondescript or undescriptive adjectives follow: *joie infinie, nuit lumineuse, jouissance exquise, œil morne, idées singulières, tendresse délicieuse, douleur horrible, paix sereine, charme tendre;* this procedure aggravated by the grouping constantly of three adjectives, three nouns, or three amplifying clauses, according to some rigid and unvarying formula, which gives a peculiar monotony to Maupassant's style. The pupil forgot the lesson in which he was told that the secret of originality was to "look at anything one wishes to describe long enough and attentively enough to discover an aspect of it which has never been seen or described by anybody else."

By the time he had reached his final phase as the chronicler of fashionable life, both his stories and his novels were more like those of Octave Feuillet than like his own earlier writings, much less those of Flaubert. It was not for nothing that his first prose was signed "Guy de Valmont," a name which he must have seen in Feuillet's *M. de Camors*, a novel which he mentions, in the preface to *Pierre et Jean*, in the same breath with *Salammbô, Adolphe, Madame Bovary, Sapho*, and *L'Assommoir*. In the end he emulated his predecessor as the purveyor of passionate fiction for society ladies so successfully that the style of Feuillet and Maupassant is often indistinguishable. When he confessed his difficulties with *Fort comme la mort*, when he laughed at himself for writing so sentimentally in *Mont-Oriol*, he was clearly conscious that he was entering a new phase of his career, and he was uncertain of himself, he who always used to possess his subject so thoroughly, who had the born story-teller's assurance in the presentation of it.

Fame, money, and an immense popularity consoled an ailing man for his lack of originality, for the loss of the old, superb strength and gusto, and his doubts were stifled when *Notre Cœur* found its appropriate outlet in the *Revue des Deux Mondes*. Here, to all his existing tricks and defects of style, his *cliché* adjectives, his repetitions of words, his recurring groups of three epithets, his sentences running to one hundred and thirty words, was added a sugary touch of boudoir philosophy which was all that was lacking to complete the conquest of his new public. His characters no longer explained themselves in action; the author explains them, and they do not carry conviction. He has no story to tell — none, that is, in which he is interested as he was interested in *Yvette*, or *Boule de Suif*, or *Bel-Ami* — and so he pads out his pages with correspondence, or with otiose discussions, or with descriptions so elaborate and off the main line of the story's progress that they burst out of his framework.

In the sheer gift of narrative lay all of Maupassant's power and charm, not in the work of stylistic revision. As he once declared, his stories were finished before he sat down to write them. The process of composition with him was exactly the reverse of Flaubert's; so much so that he could never have been touched by the practical example of Flaubert, however much he may have respected his teaching as a theory of art. The Flaubertian veneer was very thin, and did not wear well. He accepted the corrections of his first efforts without really

understanding them, as a schoolboy submits to those of
his teacher. He understood them only vaguely, and as
soon as he escaped from school, as soon as he came of
age as an author himself, he could recite the lessons
with grateful affection for the old master from whom he
had learnt them, but he could not put those methods
into practice. To have done so would have implied that
he had acquired convictions which he actually never
held. Céard, with more evidence before him than Flaubert could have had, summed him up to Goncourt by
saying that with Maupassant literature was wholly a
matter of instinct, not of reflection — in which the disciple was the direct antithesis of his Master.

His own real conception of himself was that of a
story-teller for the great masses of his fellow Frenchmen,
for whom he had a real understanding and a contemptuous affection, quite different from the cold, profound
contempt of Flaubert. The creator of M. Homais, of
Bouvard and Pécuchet, could not have seen them as
Maupassant describes them in *Sur l'eau:*

"They were commercial travellers. They talked of
everything with conviction, with authority, with mock-
ery, with contempt, and they gave me a definite impression of what the French mind is; that is, the average of
intelligence, reason, logic, and wit in France. One of
them, a huge fellow with a shock of red hair, wore a
military medal. A brave man. A little stout chap was
punning incessantly and laughing heartily at his own
jokes, without waiting for the others to see the point.
Another, with close-cropped hair, was reorganizing the
army and the state, reforming the laws and the constitu-
tion, defining his utopia as a traveller in wines. Two
others were greatly amused in telling their lucky love
adventures, their romances in the back rooms of shops
and with servant girls. And there I saw the whole of

France, the legendary, witty, restless, good-natured, and gallant France. These men were the racial types, vulgar types whom I should only have to poeticize a little in order to find the Frenchman as shown in history, that mendacious and hysterical old dame. And ours is really an amusing race, because of very special qualities which are found nowhere else."

We can see in that group the typical audience which Maupassant found, and which he interpreted no less truly than a Huysmans, a Céard, or a Zola, because of the flashes of ironic good humour which are characteristic of his healthier work. At the time he wrote down those observations his mind had been warped by suffering, and he would doubtless have seen in Verlet's reclining young lady in the Parc Monceau what he came to regard as his particular public, those "very Parisian" figures of his who are usually stereotyped automatons. He was at his best and truest as the painter of simple types, of normal life, and his fame has rested, in the last analysis, upon his irresistible appeal to the more unsophisticated French public and its counterparts everywhere. In France his position is analogous to that of the elder Dumas. He has not been the subject of much critical exegesis, and there is no satisfactory biography of him. Like Dumas, he has only to be introduced to foreign audiences and he at once captures the support of all classes of readers. There is in him the fundamental stuff of life and literature, and both poured from him in streams of prodigious energy. His active literary life lies within the brief span of ten years, and in that time he produced the twenty-nine volumes now constituting the definitive edition of his works: six novels, over three hundred stories and sketches, three books of travel, a volume of plays, and a book of verse.

If he shared to the end Flaubert's disillusioned view

of life, he never knew until the eve of his irremediable defeat that agony of sterile labour with which Flaubert's artistic conscience mocked him. He never found in the act of creating itself the all-absorbing joy which Flaubert never lost, and his compensations were of a more dangerous kind. But he had the true creative prodigality of the great masters of popular French fiction, and, had he lived, volume succeeding volume would have confronted posterity with those amazing bibliographies which stand under certain French names, from Balzac, Hugo, and Dumas, at the head of the scale, to Eugène Sue, Paul de Kock, and Ponson du Terrail, at the bottom. The best of these wrote much that was as bad as anything written by the worst, and in the worst there is always some power. None is so great that a rigid winnowing would not reduce the bulk of his writings to dimensions more worthy of his reputation and more true to the actual living part of the vast material, which would bury a lesser reputation. Maupassant, in his turn, will be subjected to selection. Already in translations that process has been at work. There will always remain of him enough to justify the faith in him which Flaubert was the first to proclaim.

"He belongs to no party and to no clique. I know as little what stirs his enthusiasm as what arouses his hate. . . . His work-table is covered with letters, perfume sachets, photographs, and coroneted notes, all the gifts and the homage of women. They pursue him everywhere, worship him, quarrel over his manuscripts, and correct his proofs. When he is working, he does it with complete equanimity, just as he eats and talks. Maupassant cannot be excited. If an intruder rings, he receives him calmly. When the visit is over, he philosophically resumes his interrupted task. . . . One may look over his shoulder at his manuscript; he does not mind. He is a writer who is never disturbed. . . . A smiling calm envelops him from head to foot. His eye has a sceptical glance, but his voice is peculiarly soft. He talks exactly as he writes. If one listens, one immediately recognizes his prose style. His conversation is cautious and deliberate. He never says a superfluous word, and seldom talks about himself. He never attacks, but his retorts are deadly. He constantly displays a remarkable calm. He never asks questions or forces himself upon one; he betrays not the slightest trace of curiosity. One does not even feel that he is observing one."

Thus Porto-Riche saw him at the height of his powers and his renown. Knowing what was behind that appearance, but had not yet thrust itself into the foreground, one must think all the more of this picture, because it explains the author of *Boule de Suif* and *La Maison Tellier*, of *Bel-Ami* and *Une Vie*. The difference between that Maupassant of 1885 and the weary paranoiac who fancied the French fleet had fired a salute of guns in his honour at Cannes, between the exuberant youth who shared his boat and Mouche with his friends and the fashionable squire of dames waiting at imaginary *rendez-vous* for marquises, while his friends laughed at the success of their practical jokes, is measured in the descending scale of his works. From these he thought he had banished all trace of his personal history, and he was morbidly opposed to all efforts to seek out the personality behind the writings. He feared that others might see and show him that which he divined in himself and against which he so vainly struggled. Were we not able, however, thus to trace the simultaneous curve of his literary career and his physical life, it would not be so easy to understand why his place in French literature is assured.

INDEX

INDEX